CELEBRATE

Traditional Ethnic
Entertaining in America

▲▲▲▲▲▲▲▲▲▲▲▲▲▲▲▲▲▲▲▲▲▲▲▲▲▲▲▲▲▲▲▲▲▲

CELEBRATE

Traditional Ethnic Entertaining in America

Hillary Davis

Principal Photographer Lois Ellen Frank

CRESCENT BOOKS
New York

A FRIEDMAN GROUP BOOK

This 1992 edition published by Crescent Books, distributed by Outlet Book Company, Inc.,
a Random House Company,
34 Engelhard Avenue, Avenel, New Jersey 07001.

ISBN 0-517-05179-6

Library of Congress Cataloging-in-Publication Data

Davis, Hillary.
    Celebrate: traditional ethnic entertaining in America /
Hillary Davis.
        p.   cm.
    "A Friedman Group book"—Verso t.p.
    Includes index.
    ISBN 0-517-05179-6 (hardcover)
    1. Festivals—United States.   2. Ethnic folklore—United States.
3. Holidays—United States.   4. Cookery, International.   I. Title.
GT4803.D38   1992
394.2'6973—dc20   91-38714
                                                            CIP

CELEBRATE:
Traditional Ethnic Entertaining in America
was prepared and produced by
Michael Friedman Publishing Group, Inc.
15 West 26th Street
New York, New York 10010

Editors: Stephen Williams and Kelly Matthews
Art Director: Jeff Batzli
Designer: Judy Morgan
Photography Editor: Ede Rothaus

Typeset by Classic Type, Inc.
Color separations by Rainbow Graphic Arts Co.
Printed and bound in Hong Kong by Leefung-Asco Printers Ltd.

8   7   6   5   4   3   2   1

For Mike Flynt

Special thanks
to Ellen Michaud

c o n t

ents

*W*hat is *Folk Entertaining?* At first,
I believed this book would show how
you could entertain in the style of, for example,
a Vietnamese-American family, an African-
American family, an Italian-American family,
a Greek-American family, or any American
family and gain insight into their way of life.

Great idea, right? Because what I've found is
that most people have been so "Americanized"
that their heritage has been allowed to fall by
the wayside.

And that's a tragedy for us all. But maybe we
shouldn't be too quick to judge. Remember that
many of the people who immigrated to this
country were leaving homes stricken by poverty
and disease. America ached for numbers of
people to work its machinery and develop the
technology for an ever-widening future. It's no
wonder that many of these destitute immigrants
wanted to leave their past behind and make a
new life. And sometimes the sheer energy it took
to establish themselves in a new culture left little

time to pay homage to the old.

My own grandfather, who was a cook on a Greek fishing boat, jumped ship while docked in New York City, changed his name from Dertewzos to Davis, and became an American as fast as he could. He wanted desperately to assimilate into this new American way of life, just like everyone else.

Unfortunately, immigrants frequently were greeted not with opportunity but with bigotry. In response, various groups banded together and settled in certain areas, which then became cities within cities and towns within towns. In some areas whole villages appeared to have been transported from one place to another. This is why we find areas like Chinatown, Little Italy, Little India, and Spanish Harlem. And why we find Native Americans still grouped on the reservations where they were once forced to live.

Today, upon entering the boundaries of these neighborhoods, you're immediately struck with the feeling that you've stepped through a cultural

time warp. And perhaps as close as one block over from where you entered, you'll find yourself walking in yet another cultural area—as is the case with Little Italy and Chinatown in New York City. It's an amazing experience.

But, even so, a somewhat disturbing problem remains. Even though there are pockets of cultural diversity, a large portion of the traditional values once held by these people seems to have been lost. Young people seem to spend much of their time trying to assimilate into an all-too-

rigid and narrow definition of America. As a young person, being different in any way can be a painful and alienating experience. And, as a result, the need to assimilate frequently subverts the idea that it's desirable to have pride in your origins.

One way to overcome this problem, however, is with food, a medium through which most people can communicate. After all, we all need to eat. And different foods allow people to sample a country's climate, religion, value system, and

traditions without feeling overwhelmed by the need to conform. Food is one of the few ways people can maintain their traditions and still feel that these particular differences are positive—not somehow debilitating or isolating.

In *Folk Entertaining* I have tried as best I can to establish a sense of what a variety of American ethnic groups are like through the foods they eat and use in rituals. Perhaps, after reading about some of the groups and sampling their foods, you'll want to learn more about their cultures.

Or, perhaps, even your own. I hope you do. And I hope, with all my heart, that you share your knowledge and pass it on to future generations with pride.

Hillary Davis
New York

▲▲▲▲▲▲▲▲▲▲▲▲▲▲▲▲

The Shaker Picnic

This meetinghouse, built in 1789 in Lebanon, New York (left),
is where Joseph Meacham and Lucy Wright chose to establish
the Shaker community.

*a*nn Lee, an unschooled English textile worker and cook who would later found the Shakers, joined the ranks of the Wardley Society, a group of American dissenters led by Quaker tailors, in 1758. These religious enthusiasts had fallen into the hands of a radical group of Calvinists known as the French prophets, or Camisards. They took easily to fasting, trances, prophecies, heavenly voices, and other signs of godly favor, while the "mighty shakes" induced by their spiritual fervor led them to be called the "Shaking Quakers" or "Shakers."

Lee married and had four children, all of whom died. She ultimately came to see this as a divine judgment against her for conceiving them in the first place. This led her to believe that sex was a sin—that even men and women living together was a sin. Her advocacy of this strict and unusual belief eventually led to her imprisonment. From prison she claimed that Christ told her to go forth and preach the gospel of a "stainless life."

Personal visions told her a chosen people were waiting for her. Out of prison, she left her husband and with eight followers went to Watervliet, New York, on May 10, 1776, where she established the Shaker Church and lived until she died in 1784.

Joseph Meacham was her first male apostle, while Lucy Wright was his female equivalent. In 1787, Meacham and Wright felt that it was time for all true Shakers to withdraw from the world and form a community in Lebanon, New York, where a meetinghouse was to be built by 1789.

Since this community adhered to Mother Ann's ban on sex, membership was maintained by converting outsiders. New members were frequently recruited through picnics to which the outsiders from the "world" were invited. And the world came. Because the Shakers used herbs and spices extensively, their dishes were more exotic than other types of American cooking. Foods were home-grown, and serving quality food—to themselves as well as others—was a sacred commitment of the Shakers that resulted in outstanding meals.

Vegetables and fruits were grown in vast quantities and varieties. Immaculately clean dairies supplied milk, cream, and cheeses. Hickory nuts, walnuts, and butternuts were in plentiful supply. Bees supplied honey, and maple trees yielded syrup.

Such industry and fruitfulness on the farm made it logical to avoid waste in the kitchen, and "Shaker your plate"—eat it all —became an admonition from a people to whom waste was an affront to God. It was even a duty of the deacons and deaconesses to see that suitable food was provided for the communal family and to ensure that food was cooked with "good economy."

Shaker cooking, like their furniture, architecture, and dress, expressed genuine simplicity, excellent quality, and resourceful imaginations. Explicit rules were followed when using recipes, and perfection was demanded.

The Shakers even learned to apply scientific methods to their cooking. Because they worked with vast amounts of food, they had to establish weights, measures, and relative amounts. They constantly thought in terms of a balanced diet and were far ahead of their time in their knowledge of nutrition and food values. In well-equipped nursing houses and infirmaries, they were the ones responsible for prescribing healing diets.

Etiquette in the dining room was strict. All conversation was forbidden, since talking prolonged mealtimes and that prolonged the work involved. The "sisters" prepared and served the food, and when someone wanted something, they would beckon to one of the sisters and whisper their need.

Meals were served punctually: breakfast one and a half hours after rising, dinner at high noon, supper at six o'clock. When everyone was satisfied, they rose at the signal of the head elder, fell upon their knees, thanked God for their bounty, and silently filed out of the dining room.

Suppers at Christmas and on the Sabbath were sumptuous meals for which roast fowl, pies, cakes, and preserves were prepared. In season, vegetables were harvested within the hour. Pies were shortened with sweet cream and filled with fresh fruit.

From 1837 to 1847, the Shaker community banned meat and promoted vegetarianism. Even though they realized that the abundant diet of grains, vegetables, fruits, eggs, and milk products had answered every physiological need, vegetarianism didn't last.

Perhaps that was due to the bounty of game and farm animals available to the Shakers. Fish of all types abounded in the neighboring lakes and streams, and chickens were also abundant. Beef was served at breakfast and dinner, while ham was frequently a feature of supper. In fact, the Shakers were known for raising the English Berkshire hog.

The Shakers were also excellent horticulturalists who developed new and better varieties of vegetables. Steaming, as opposed to boiling, was the favored cooking method since boiling was thought to leach out beneficial natural salts.

Picnics were of special interest to the Shakers since they used them to attract new members. But they were also the centerpiece of inter-Shaker socializing. At least once a year, each Shaker community visited the others in order to maintain a sense of unity. And since they had little contact with the outside world, visits and picnics also gave them a chance to move beyond their self-made walls and see different areas of the country. They even prepared special "traveling" foods just for this purpose. Here are some of the foods they'd be sure to include.

The Shaker Picnic

MENU

Cold Pork Pie · Pickled Oysters
Potato Salad · Coffee Spice Cake

Known for raising the English Berkshire hog, the Shakers'

cold pork pies were often the centerpieces of picnics aimed

at recruiting new members.

Cold Pork Pie

**2¹/₂ pounds pork tenderloin, cubed into
    ¹/₂-inch pieces**

³/₄ pound cubed lean salt pork

8 cloves garlic, crushed

¹/₂ teaspoon whole black peppercorns

1 tablespoon fresh rosemary, chopped

1 medium onion, finely minced

**Salt and freshly ground black pepper
    (to taste)**

1 cup vegetable shortening

1³/₄ cups water

4 cups all-purpose flour

1 teaspoon salt

1 large egg, beaten

2 tablespoons unflavored gelatin

2 tablespoons Calvados

Preheat oven to 400°F. In a 3-quart saucepan, combine pork and salt pork with enough water to cover. Add garlic, peppercorns, rosemary, onion, and salt and pepper. Bring to boil over high heat, reduce heat to medium, and simmer, covered, about 1 hour or until meat is quite tender. Drain meat, strain, and reserve stock.

To make hot water pastry, bring shortening and water to a boil in a 4-quart saucepan. In a separate large mixing bowl, sift together the flour and salt. Stir this into the lard mixture. When cool enough to handle, turn the dough out onto a lightly floured surface and knead for a few minutes. If the dough gets too cold, it will become crumbly and difficult to manage. Reserve one-quarter of the pie pastry for the top. Use a deep 2-quart pie plate. Line the bottom and the sides of the pan by patting the dough into place. Fill the lined pan with the pork mixture. Roll out top and cover pie. Cut a hole 1-inch in diameter in the center. Brush with the beaten egg.

Bake in the oven on center shelf for 1¹/₂ to 2 hours or more, until the crust is golden but not brown. To keep the crust from browning too much, cover with aluminum foil. About 40 minutes before the pie is done, take the pork stock and add a little of it to unflavored gelatin. When the gelatin is completely dissolved, return it to the remaining stock and add the Calvados. When pie is properly baked, add as much of the stock mixture as it will hold, pouring it through a funnel into the hole cut out of the pie top. Cool the pie completely.

Serves 6 to 8.

*A seemingly unusual element in the
Shaker diet, oysters found their way into
the Shakers' cuisine. Now delicacies, these
will add a wonderful dimension to
anyone's table—be it outside or in.*

Pickled Oysters

1 teaspoon ground allspice

1 teaspoon ground cloves

1 teaspoon ground mace

1/2 teaspoon cinnamon

1 teaspoon sugar

2 cups champagne vinegar

2 cups large fresh oysters, shelled and cleaned

In a 2-quart saucepan, combine spices and sugar together with the vinegar over high heat. Bring to a boil. Reduce to a simmer, and cook 2 to 3 minutes. Place in refrigerator until well chilled. When cold, add oysters. Marinate overnight. The following day bring to a boil for 1 minute. Chill completely.

Serves 8.

Potato Salad

3 pounds new potatoes, boiled, drained, and thinly sliced

1 medium onion, finely chopped

1/4 cup fresh chives, chopped

1/2 cup chopped celery

1 tablespoon fresh thyme, chopped

12 thinly sliced radishes

3 tablespoons Dijon-style mustard

1/2 cup mayonnaise

1/4 cup sweet pickle relish

1/8 teaspoon cayenne pepper

1 teaspoon salt

1 teaspoon freshly ground black pepper

6 hard-boiled eggs, quartered

Toss potatoes, onions, chives, celery, thyme, and radishes together in large bowl. In a small bowl, mix the Dijon mustard, mayonnaise, relish, cayenne pepper, and salt and pepper, and blend well. Add this to the potatoes and toss to coat evenly. To serve, line a large wooden bowl with lettuce leaves. Spoon in the potato salad and garnish with quartered eggs.

Serves 6 to 8.

Coffee Spice Cake

1 cup butter

1/2 cup granulated sugar

2 large eggs, well beaten

1 cup molasses

4 cups all-purpose flour

1 1/2 tablespoons baking powder

1 teaspoon ground cinnamon

2 teaspoons ground ginger

2 teaspoons ground nutmeg

1 cup cold Italian espresso coffee

1 cup currants

Preheat oven to 350°F. Using an electric mixer, cream butter and gradually add sugar. Add eggs and molasses. In a separate bowl, sift together all the dry ingredients. Add slowly, in 3 to 4 batches, alternating with the cold coffee until well mixed. Stir in the currants until evenly distributed.

Butter and flour two deep 8-inch- or 9-inch-square cake pans. Bake 45 minutes to 1 hour until a knife inserted in the center comes out clean. Cool completely on a wire rack. Cut each cake into 4 to 5 pieces.

Serves 8 to 10.

Mardi Gras

During Mardi Gras, the streets of New Orleans are packed
with enthusiastic party-goers who shout the traditional chants to
the costumed figures on the floats.

*m*ardi Gras, arguably the nation's wildest party, began when several young men returned to New Orleans in 1827 after completing their educations in Paris and decided to march through the city on *mardi gras* (literally, "fat Tuesday"), the day before Lent.

By 1857, one of the New Orleans newspapers was quoted as saying that Mardi Gras had degenerated into a vulgar, tasteless, and spiritless event that, the newspapers hoped, would just go away.

It didn't. Between nine and ten o'clock on the night of Mardi Gras, 1857, an unusual, never-before-seen, and never-to-be-forgotten procession issued from some unknown rendezvous, and the first stage in the evolution of Mardi Gras as we know it began. The procession was the first time the Mystick Krewe of Comus had paraded at night. A flamboyant tradition had begun.

There are now more than sixty Mardi Gras organizations in New Orleans, but according to admittedly biased sources, the Rex association—formed in 1872 to provide entertainment for Grand Duke Alex of Russia—has become the most important. The association's monarch, "Rex," is king of the carnival.

Each year, the identity of Rex is kept a secret, even from friends and family, until the morning of Mardi Gras. The degree of respect bestowed on him, and to a lesser degree to the kings of the other organizations, is truly amazing. He is treated as royalty, toasted by the mayor, and his parade is the highlight of the day. As allegorical floats manned by masked knights slowly wind their way through the narrow streets of the Vieux Carré, enthusiastic Mardi Gras–goers shout the traditional chants to the costumed figures on the floats, such as, "Throw me something, mistah!" All sorts of odds and ends and knickknacks are thrown to the crowds that, even though they are of little monetary value, are sought after with as much enthusiasm as is shown for the event itself.

Besides the floats, dancers, marching groups, and innumerable bands, New Orleans is filled with ordinary citizens who become quite extraordinary for Mardi Gras. They are decked out in a vast array of unusual costumes that range from circus clowns to fantastic beasts. On Canal Street you might see a group of young men wearing the hide of an animal while lugging around a spit that holds a whole roasted pig. If they feel so inclined, these same young men might even sit on a curb while tearing their pig apart. In the eyes of many, the spirit of Mardi Gras remains as much in the spontaneous street theater as in the elaborate parades.

These festivals open officially around mid-February with the Twelfth Night Reveler's Ball, and come to a close at the final ball on Mardi Gras night. Here's a sampling of foods you might expect to eat at a late-night Cajun-style supper.

Mardi Gras

MENU

Shrimp and Okra Gumbo
Smoked Sausage in Red Gravy
Blackened Swordfish
Fried Green Tomatoes
Bread Pudding with Bourbon Sauce

Shrimp and Okra Gumbo

1¹/₂ pounds shrimp, peeled and deveined

1 tablespoon plus ¹/₂ teaspoon kosher salt

1 teaspoon cayenne pepper

3 large cloves garlic, crushed

1 cup finely minced red onion

¹/₄ cup finely chopped green bell pepper

4 tablespoons butter

¹/₄ cup flour

³/₄ pound fresh okra, sliced in ¹/₄-inch pieces

1 cup peeled, seeded, and chopped tomatoes

1 tablespoon salt

1¹/₄ quarts fish broth

³/₄ cup minced scallions

¹/₂ teaspoon gumbo filé (available in specialty stores)

In a small bowl, combine the shrimp, ¹/₂ teaspoon salt, cayenne pepper, and garlic. Toss to coat. Cover with plastic wrap and refrigerate until ready to use. In a medium-size bowl, combine the onions with the bell pepper; set aside. Meanwhile, in a large 1-quart saucepan, melt 2 tablespoons butter over medium-high heat. When it starts to bubble, add the flour all at once and stir constantly with a wooden spoon for 3 to 5 minutes until it starts to take on a toasted brown color and has a nutty smell. Add the onions and the green pepper, stirring to blend well. Reserve.

In a 6-quart saucepan or Dutch oven, combine the remaining 2 tablespoons butter with the okra, tomatoes, and salt. Place over high heat and cook about 20 minutes, stirring frequently. Add ¹/₂ cup fish stock and continue cooking 5 to 10 minutes longer. Add 2 more cups of the stock, and stir and scrape bottom of pan until all sediment is dissolved. Bring the stock to a boil, adding the cooked flour-butter mixture slowly into the boiling stock while stirring with a wire whisk. Reduce heat and simmer 40 minutes. Stir in scallions and gumbo filé. Add shrimp. Stir and cook until shrimp are pink and just tender. Be careful not to overcook.
Serves 8.

Mention Louisiana cooking and the first things that come to mind are blackened meat and fish (that's swordfish on the right) and gumbo (left). These highly seasoned foods with their unique ingredients are what make Cajun and Creole cuisines distinctive.

Smoked Sausage in Red Gravy

3 tablespoons butter

³/₄ pound Polish kielbasa, cut into 2-inch pieces

1¹/₂ cups thinly sliced onion

3 cups beef broth

¹/₄ teaspoon salt

³/₄ teaspoon cayenne pepper

¹/₄ cup finely chopped celery

¹/₂ cup green bell pepper, chopped

3 cloves garlic, minced

1 8-ounce can prepared tomato sauce

¹/₄ cup finely chopped parsley

¹/₂ cup finely minced scallions

In a heavy-duty saucepan, melt butter over high heat. When butter begins to brown, add the sausage and cover. Cook, without stirring, until sausage is well browned on bottom, about 7 to 10 minutes. Turn sausage over and add the onion. Re-cover and cook an additional 7 to 10 minutes without stirring, until onion and sausage are well browned and there is a lot of brown sediment. Add ³/₄ cup of beef broth and scrape the bottom of the pan clean. Add salt, cayenne pepper, celery, bell pepper, and garlic, stirring well. Cover and cook about 15 minutes over medium heat. Stir in tomato sauce, parsley, scallions, and remaining beef stock. Bring to a boil over high heat. Reduce heat to low and simmer 15 minutes longer. Serve over white rice. *Serves 8.*

Blackened Swordfish

6 to 8 8-ounce swordfish steaks

1 stick butter, melted and kept warm in an 8-inch skillet

1 tablespoon paprika

2½ teaspoons salt

1 teaspoon onion powder

1 teaspoon cayenne pepper

1 teaspoon garlic powder

½ teaspoon white pepper

½ teaspoon ground black pepper

1 teaspoon Herbes de Provence .

2 teaspoons oregano

In a small bowl, combine herbs and spices. Mix well. Heat a cast-iron skillet over high heat for 7 minutes until extremely hot. Brush each side of the swordfish with the melted butter. Sprinkle seasoning mix on both sides. Place the swordfish in the hot skillet one steak at a time. Cover and cook 2 minutes or until a crust forms on the underside. Turn fish and cook, covered, an additional 2 minutes. Remove to a serving platter and keep warm in the oven while repeating this procedure with the other fish. Be sure to wipe out the pan each time you cook a piece of fish, and do not place cooked fish on top of one another, since this will cause the crust to become soft.

Serves 6 to 8.

Fried Green Tomatoes

5 to 6 very green tomatoes

½ cup all-purpose flour

3 tablespoons baking powder

2 cups vegetable oil for frying

Seasoning Mix:

1 tablespoon black pepper

1 teaspoon salt

½ teaspoon cayenne pepper

1 teaspoon garlic powder

Slice tomatoes into ¼-inch slices. Remove core end and bottom end. Place slices on a flat surface in one layer. Combine seasonings together in a small bowl and sprinkle evenly over all tomato slices. Sift together flour and baking powder into a shallow pan or plate. In a large 12-inch skillet, heat 1 inch of oil over medium-high heat. Dredge each tomato slice thoroughly in the flour and fry slices in a single layer for 3 to 5 minutes on each side or until golden brown. Remove from pan and drain on a paper towel. Repeat procedure until all slices are done.

Serves 6 to 8.

Bread Pudding with Bourbon Sauce

1 stick unsalted butter, at room temperature

$^1/_2$ cup sugar

2 12-ounce cans evaporated skim milk

3 eggs

2 teaspoons vanilla extract

1 teaspoon ground cinnamon

$^1/_2$ teaspoon ground nutmeg

$^1/_2$ teaspoon ground ginger

$^1/_2$ teaspoon salt

$^1/_4$ teaspoon cream of tartar

$^1/_2$ cup raisins

7 to 8 pieces of stale white bread, toasted

Preheat oven to 450°F. In a large mixing bowl, combine the butter and the sugar and beat with an electric mixer on medium speed until creamed and well blended. Scrape down the sides of the bowl with a rubber spatula. Add milk, eggs, vanilla, cinnamon, nutmeg, ginger, salt, and cream of tartar. Beat for 3 minutes on low speed until ingredients are well blended. Dust raisins with a little flour and fold into batter.

Evenly line the bottom of an ungreased 8×8-inch baking pan with the toasted bread. Pour the batter over the bread and let it sit for about 1 hour, pressing down the pieces of bread that float to the top. Bake 20 to 25 minutes or until pudding is well browned and jiggles like a bowl of jelly in the center when shaken back and forth. Serve with Bourbon Sauce (recipe follows).

Serves 6 to 8.

Bourbon Sauce

$1^1/_2$ cups water

$^1/_2$ cup bourbon

$^1/_4$ cup sugar

$^1/_8$ teaspoon salt

2 tablespoons melted butter

2 teaspoons flour

2 teaspoons grated lemon rind

In a 1-quart saucepan, combine water, bourbon, sugar, and salt over high heat. Bring to a boil and cook 15 minutes. In another saucepan, combine melted butter and flour until well blended. Slowly, with a wire whisk, add the hot sauce to the butter-flour mixture. Stir and cook over high heat until it boils. Remove from heat and stir in lemon rind.

Makes 2 cups.

Bread pudding is a wonderfully creative—and delicious—way of using old bread. Not only is it a very simple and homey dessert, but with the addition of a sauce, it can be transformed into a dish special enough for guests.

The Jewish Seder

The Jewish Passover seder is a traditional celebration recognizing

freedom, religious devotion, and family solidarity. Passover

commemorates the freeing of the Jews from slavery in Egypt.

the various elements of the Jewish Passover seder—the lamb, the unleavened bread, the household celebration, and the story of the Jews' deliverance out of slavery in Egypt—melds into a festival much greater than the sum of its parts. What is traditionally a celebration of freedom, religious devotion, and respect for law and life is also a time of family and community solidarity.

It's even a time of spring renewal. Part of the Passover observances resemble seasonal festivals, when a new agricultural cycle is marked by a communal meal in which the purity and perfection of the food are of paramount importance.

According to tradition, three thousand years ago the Jewish people were enslaved by the Egyptians who were then under the rule of the pharoah Ramses II. Their bitter and oppressive servitude showed no signs of subsiding until, as described in the twelfth chapter of the Book of Exodus, God instructed Moses, a shepherd, to

approach the pharoah and demand freedom for his people. As Moses cried out, "Let my people go," the pharoah scoffed at his plea. God responded with a series of horrific plagues, but it wasn't until the last, the slaying of the firstborn in every house, that the pharoah was convinced to free the Jews, who had marked their doors with lamb's blood so the Angel of Death would "pass over" them.

When the Egyptian pharaoh released the Jews from bondage, they had to leave quickly, taking unleavened bread with them because they had no time to wait for it to rise. Today the eating of unleavened bread—matzo—is a symbolic ritual that celebrates the cooperation of man and God in the establishment of freedom and the rejection of bondage and idolatry.

One of the most important ordinances of Passover is the obligation to retell the story of the exodus from Egypt and to explain the symbols of the Passover meal to each succeeding generation. The

exchange between the generations takes place at dinner in a ceremony known as the seder ("order" or "procedure"). The seder has, in fact, come to be the central focus of the Passover celebration.

During the seder, various foods symbolizing the experiences of the Israelites in Egypt are used. The foods include a roasted shank bone of lamb (to be viewed but not eaten), which represents the sacrifice of the lamb; matzo, the unleavened bread; bitter herbs, such as horseradish to commemorate the bitterness of slavery; charoset, a mixture of apples, nuts, raisins, and cinnamon, which represents the mortar the Israelites used to make bricks in Egypt; parsley and hard-boiled eggs, to suggest the greenery and renewal of life in springtime; and saltwater, which represents the tears of the Israelite slaves (the parsley and egg are dipped in the saltwater).

Most of the condiments are adapted from a Roman meal. Foods are eaten in

The seder has, in fact, come to be the central focus of the Passover

celebration. During the seder, various foods are used to symbolize

the experience of the Israelites in Egypt.

THE JEWISH SEDER 31

a prescribed order as explanations of their meanings are heard. There may also be informal discussion and recitations of blessings. A festive main course is eaten in the middle of the seder, usually a simply done chicken or pot roast, and four glasses of wine are drunk with appropriate blessings.

An extra wineglass is filled and placed on the table for the prophet Elijah, who is invited but not present—although everyone attending the seder knows that he might arrive any day and bring the Messiah with him. The invitation to Elijah is thus an expression of hope—a look to future redemption with the knowledge that an exodus into a better way of life, one of peace and brotherhood, is still possible.

The format of the seder is dictated by a book, known as the Haggadah, which the participants read together. Haggadah ("telling" or "narrative") is a word that frequently refers to Jewish legend in general. The Passover Haggadah contains the story of the exodus as it was enhanced by legend. It also contains songs, blessings, psalms, and above all, the "Four Questions." The questions are begun by first asking, "Why is this night different from all other nights?" The four questions then posed by the youngest member of the family are answered by the father and they explain the symbolism within the holiday.

Usually the head of the family takes a piece of matzo wrapped in a napkin and hides it away to be searched for by the children. There's a prize for the finder. This hidden matzo is called *afikomen*, a term derived from the Greek word *epikomen*, which is commonly translated as "dessert."

The seder also includes the parable of the "Four Sons," a story in which four types of children—wise, wicked, simple, and inarticulate—ask the meaning of Passover. Included is the "Litany of Wonders," a retelling of the miraculous deeds performed by God from the Passover through the Covenant at Mount Sinai to the entry into a new land. Each deed is answered by the cry, *"Dayenu!"* ("It would have sufficed us!")

Also during the seder, the participants recite the Hallel, or psalms of praise, which are punctuated by the exclamation, "Hallelujah!"

Here is a sampling of foods that might be served at a modern-day seder.

The Jewish Seder

MENU

My Mother's Matzo Ball Soup

Brisket of Beef with Dried Fruits

Candied Carrots · Charoset

Sponge Cake with Strawberry Sauce

My Mother's Matzo Ball Soup

2 tablespoons chicken fat

2 eggs, lightly beaten

2 cloves garlic, crushed

2 tablespoons fresh parsley, chopped

$^1/_2$ teaspoon salt

$^1/_4$ teaspoon ground white pepper

$^3/_4$ cup matzo cracker crumbs

6 cups chicken stock or canned chicken broth

Cream chicken fat in a bowl; add eggs, garlic, parsley, salt, pepper, and enough cracker crumbs to make a soft dough. Cover and refrigerate for 1 to 2 hours. Bring chicken stock to boil over high heat. Make small 1-inch balls from the chilled dough. Drop into the boiling stock and cook about 15 minutes. Serve immediately. *Serves 6.*

It doesn't have to be Passover to make matzo ball soup. Every once in a while, my mother would get the urge, and as a child, I had so much fun watching the matzo balls float in the rich smelling chicken broth. It was a real treat for me then—and still is now.

Often the seder meal concludes simply, with a broiled chicken or boiled brisket of beef. This recipe for a classic brisket is given an interesting twist by adding dried fruits.

Brisket of Beef with Dried Fruits

1 3-pound brisket of beef

1 medium onion, chopped

1 teaspoon salt

$^1/_2$ teaspoon ground black pepper

1 tablespoon fresh ginger, grated

6 cloves

$^1/_2$ cup dried apricots

$^1/_2$ cup dried prunes

$^1/_4$ cup dried currants

$1^1/_2$ pounds all-purpose potatoes, peeled and cut into $^1/_4$-inch cubes

$^1/_4$ cup butter

$^1/_4$ cup flour

2 tablespoons sugar

$^1/_2$ cup red wine

Preheat oven to 375°F. Put the beef and onion in a heavy-duty enamel casserole dish. Fill the dish with boiling water to cover beef. Bring to a boil over high heat. Skim the surface. Season with salt, pepper, and spices. Cover casserole, reduce heat to low, and simmer 30 minutes. While the meat is cooking, combine the fruits in a 1-quart saucepan with enough water to cover and cook over medium heat. Simmer 30 minutes. Drain and reserve cooking liquid. Add the fruits and potatoes to the casserole and simmer until the potatoes are tender, about 10 to 15 minutes.

In a 1-quart saucepan, melt butter over medium heat. Add flour and stir constantly 3 to 5 minutes or until the mixture leaves the bottom of the pan and is lightly browned. Add reserved fruit liquid and continue stirring until the sauce thickens. Then add sugar and red wine. Stir until the sauce is smooth. Keep warm. When the potatoes are nearly tender, add the sauce. Put casserole in oven and cook until the meat is very tender, 30 to 40 minutes.

Serves 6.

Candied Carrots

2 pounds carrots

1 cup brown sugar

2 tablespoons pareve margarine

Wash and scrape carrots and cut into ¼-inch-thick slices. Steam carrots for 20 to 30 minutes until tender. Drain and measure 1 cup of the cooking liquid. Add this liquid and the brown sugar and margarine

to a pot. Bring to a boil, and stir until the margarine is melted and the sugar is dissolved, then turn down to simmer for 10 minutes. Add carrots and cook for 10 minutes.

Serves 4 to 6.

Charoset
(Chopped Apples, Dates, and Walnuts)

1 apple, quartered, cored, and peeled

½ cup finely chopped walnuts

¼ cup chopped dates

2 tablespoons honey

2 tablespoons sweet grape wine

½ teaspoon cinnamon

Finely chop apple and add to a small bowl. Add remaining ingredients and combine well.

Makes 1¼ cups.

Sponge Cake with Strawberry Sauce

7 eggs

1½ cups sugar

2 tablespoons lemon juice

1½ teaspoons lemon rind

¾ cup potato starch, sifted twice

Dash salt

Separate 6 of the eggs. Into a bowl with the 6 yolks, add the remaining whole egg and beat with an electric beater until light and fluffy. Gradually add the sugar, lemon juice, and lemon rind to the egg mix. Beat constantly. Then add the potato starch, also beating constantly.

Beat the 6 egg whites until stiff. Gently fold the beaten whites into the potato-starch mixture. Pour this slowly into an ungreased 10-inch tube pan. Bake at 350°F for 50 minutes.

Invert cake and allow to cool in pan. Remove from pan when cool. Serve with Strawberry Sauce (recipe follows).

Makes 1 sponge cake.

Strawberry Sauce

1 pint fresh or frozen strawberries

¼ cup water

2 tablespoons sugar

Wash and hull strawberries if fresh. Add to a small pot with the water and bring to a boil. Cook several minutes. Then add to a blender with the sugar and puree.

Makes 2 cups of sauce.

Chinese New Year

The Chinese New Year is celebrated in many cities across the
United States. At this celebration in lower Manhattan (above),
the sounds of gongs, cymbals, and firecrackers permeate the air:
Noise and light are supposed to drive away evil spirits.

*t*he Chinese New Year, which is widely celebrated by Chinese Americans, takes place in either January, February, or March, according to the Chinese calendar. The Chinese first brought their rich new year's traditions to the United States, which they called *Mei Kwok,* or Beautiful Land, during the 1850s. The first Chinese in America were almost all males, recruited by companies who wanted them as laborers to build the railroads and to mine for gold. Political and economic conditions were bad for many people in China at the time, and many had great incentive to work in America, where they thought they might find riches—or at least more wealth than they would have in China.

Life was not easy for the 18,000 or so Chinese men who had arrived on the West Coast by 1852. The gold-digging forty-niners, mostly European Americans, held many racist views of the Chinese and forced Chinese men to live in ghettos.

Because there were no women or children allowed, the groups of men were referred to as "bachelor societies." Eventually, discriminatory taxes and immigration laws made it difficult for Chinese people to mine, and some began to make their living from fishing, farming, and milling.

The movement of Chinese people to America, and the growth of the Chinese American population in the century and a half that followed this initial migration have only strengthened traditions in this country. Today the Chinese New Year is celebrated with great enthusiasm throughout the United States.

To the Chinese, the new year is a time for a fresh start. It begins with a new moon and ends with the Feast of Lanterns two weeks later when the moon is full. The celebrations, however, can last up to a month. Some families observe the new year privately, but often, especially in large Chinese American communities, there are gala festivities in which hundreds of peo-

ple take part.

Anyone who has ever witnessed a Chinese New Year knows that the sounds from gongs, cymbals, drums, and firecrackers permeate the celebration—noise and light are supposed to drive away the evil spirits that have accumulated throughout the year. The firecrackers are always red, which is the traditional color of good omens.

The highlight of a new year's celebration is, of course, the dragon parade. The golden dragon is one of four divine creatures to the Chinese. The others are the unicorn, the phoenix, and the tortoise. They are all responsible for dispelling the bad spirits of ancient times. The dragon, the most favored of the four, is worshiped as the living representation of the rivers, lakes, and seas. Its legendary appearance combines the head of a camel, the horns of a deer, the neck of a snake, the claws of a hawk, the belly of a frog, and the scales of a fish.

▲▲▲▲▲▲▲▲▲▲▲▲▲▲▲

According to traditional beliefs, just before the new year the god of the kitchen is sent to heaven to report the events of the year that has just gone by. He returns on New Year's Eve, which is celebrated with a bountiful dinner.

Several weeks before New Year's Day arrives, homes are brightened by pots of colorful flowers, such as azaleas and hyacinths. And perhaps the most pervasive tradition is to adorn interiors with baskets of oranges, along with plates of candied fruits and roasted melon seeds.

Whatever you decide to cook for a Chinese New Year, there are certain traditions. A New Year's celebration must include "long life" noodles, fish for prosperity, fruits to symbolize the coming of spring, and enough food to show that life is rich and bountiful. Lots of Chinese families also put out snacks and desserts.

Chinese parents give their children gifts of money tucked into bright red envelopes —something to keep in mind if you plan on celebrating the new year and decorating your own holiday table. Try tucking a shiny new penny (or, to keep up with the times, a dollar bill) or a pair of chopsticks into the envelopes for your guests to take home. Ultimately, the overall feeling of this holiday should be one of joy and prosperity.

Here are a few recipes to start your new year off right.

▲▲▲▲▲▲▲▲▲▲▲▲▲▲▲▲▲▲▲▲▲▲▲

Chinese New Year

M E N U

Long Life Spinach Noodles
Fragrant Duck · Dragon Fish
Sweet and Sour Sauce · Spring Rolls
Litchi Nut Fruit Dessert

The Chinese New Year rejoices in the beginning of spring and celebrates a long life filled with good fortune and prosperity. These long life spinach noodles symbolize just that—a long life.

Long Life Spinach Noodles

2 cups fresh spinach

¹/₃ cup water

4 cups all-purpose flour

2 large eggs, lightly beaten

1 teaspoon salt

1 cup cornstarch

2 quarts water plus 3 cups cold water

2 tablespoons vegetable oil

Wash spinach thoroughly, cut off and discard stems, and place in the bowl of a food processor or blender. Add ¹/₃ cup water, and using the metal blade, process until spinach is finely chopped. Strain the mixture through a fine sieve into a small bowl, squeezing out as much of the liquid as possible. Discard the pulp and set the juice aside.

Mound flour in a large mixing bowl or on a work surface. Make a deep well in the center and pour in spinach juice, eggs, and salt. Using a fork, mix ingredients thoroughly and then knead dough by hand until it forms a stiff ball. Cover with a damp cloth and let it rest about 10 minutes.

Place cornstarch in a double-thick piece of cheesecloth, and dust your surface lightly with it. Dust the dough and the rolling pin with the cornstarch as well to prevent sticking. Roll out the dough into an approximately ¹/₂-inch-thick rectangle. A pasta machine is the ideal tool for doing this. Dust with more cornstarch and continue rolling out the dough until it is ¹/₁₆ inch thick. Dust with more cornstarch and fold the dough onto itself as if to make pleats, or roll it up like a jelly roll. With a very sharp knife cut across the pleats or roll, making ¹/₁₆-inch strips. Carefully lift up the top layer of the dough strips and unfold.

Bring 2 quarts of water to a boil in a large pot. Add noodles, stirring constantly to keep the dough from sticking, until it reaches a second boil. At this point, pour in the 3 cups of cold water, then return to a third boil. Remove from heat, pour noodles through a colander, rinse under cold water, and drain well. Mix with vegetable oil to serve.

Serves 6 to 8.

Fragrant Duck

1 4- to 5-pound fresh or frozen duck

Chinese parsley

5 to 6 small scallions, minced

¹/₄ cup fresh gingerroot, chopped

5 medium cloves garlic, crushed

2 star anise (available at Oriental markets)

3 tablespoons dry sherry

¹/₄ cup black soy sauce

2 tablespoons honey

2 tablespoons Szechuan peppercorns

4 tablespoons salt

In a small bowl combine all the marinade ingredients and blend well. Rub duck inside and out with the marinade, cover, and refrigerate overnight.

Place duck on rack inside a steamer large enough to hold it. Cover and steam over boiling water for 1 hour or until juices run clear when the thigh is pierced with a knife. When done, remove duck from steamer. Discard the spices clinging to the duck. Refrigerate duck until well chilled.

With a pair of poultry shears cut cold duck into sections, then cut through the bone into ¹/₂-inch-thick slices. Arrange decoratively on a platter and garnish generously with Chinese parsley.

Serves 8 to 10.

Dragon fish, symbolizing happiness and prosperity,

is usually served at large banquets or on special occasions,

but since it's so easy to prepare, why wait?

Dragon Fish

1 4- to 5-pound whole red snapper, cleaned

Salt

Batter:

1 cup all-purpose flour

1 cup cornstarch

1¹/₂ cups cold water

1 tablespoon vegetable oil

1 quart vegetable oil for frying

8 to 10 lemon wedges

Remove fish head and reserve. Make an incision running down the length of the spine.

Combine batter in a large bowl and blend well. In a large, high-sided pot or sauté pan, heat oil over medium-high heat until the temperature registers 350°F on a deep-fat-fry thermometer. Coat fish head with batter and deep fry in hot oil until golden brown. Remove with tongs to a platter lined with paper towels. Drain well and reserve. Allow oil temperature to return to 350°F. Holding the fish by the tail, dip it into the batter and make certain to coat well. Let the excess batter drip back into the bowl. Slowly immerse fish in hot oil and deep fry, basting occasionally and turning so that the oil cooks the whole fish. Fry for about 8 minutes or until golden brown. With a strainer, remove fish and drain on plate lined with paper towels. Arrange fish with its head on the platter. Surround with lemon wedges and serve with Sweet and Sour Sauce (recipe follows).

Serves 8 to 10.

Sweet and Sour Sauce

¹/₄ cup unsweetened pineapple juice

¹/₂ cup freshly squeezed orange juice

Juice from two limes

2 tablespoons fresh gingerroot, grated

1 cup catsup

³/₄ cup rice wine vinegar

2 cups water

2 tablespoons cornstarch made into a paste with cold water

In a saucepan over medium-high heat, combine all the ingredients except the cornstarch. Blend well. Bring to boil, reduce the heat to low, and simmer 5 minutes. Add enough cornstarch to thicken sauce and cook about 1 minute longer. Season with salt and pepper, if desired.

Makes 4¹/₂ to 5 cups.

It seems appropriate that spring rolls would make their way

into a Chinese New Year menu. For a different twist, try using

small wonton wrappers for bite-size spring rolls—

they're great to serve as hors d'oeuvres.

Spring Rolls

2 tablespoons vegetable oil

1 minced scallion

¼ cup cooked shrimp, minced

¼ cup cooked, shredded pork, from barbecued spareribs

1 large stalk celery, finely chopped

4 dried black mushrooms, reconstituted in 1 cup boiling water and then chopped

2 cups white cabbage, finely shredded

1 cup fresh bean sprouts

½ cup julienned bamboo shoots

2 tablespoons dry sherry

¼ teaspoon Chinese five-spice powder

1 teaspoon salt

2 teaspoons sesame oil

8 to 10 spring roll or egg roll wrappers

1 quart vegetable oil for frying

In a wok or 12-inch frying pan, add oil, and heat over high heat. When hot, add scallion and cook, stirring constantly, for 30 seconds. Add shrimp and pork, and cook for 1 minute. Stir in vegetables, and sprinkle with sherry, spice powder, and salt. Remove from heat when vegetables are cooked but not mushy. Drain in a colander until completely cooled. Stir in sesame oil.

Place egg roll wrapper with one point toward you. Put about 3 tablespoons of filling in center of wrapper. Then, taking the corner closest to you, bring it over the filling. Fold over right and left corners so that they meet in the middle. Then roll up jelly-roll style and seal the final corner with a little water. Cover each egg roll with plastic wrap to prevent it from drying out.

In a large pot or wok, heat vegetable oil until it reaches 350°F on a deep-fat-fry thermometer. Carefully fry 4 to 5 rolls at a time for about 3 minutes or until nicely browned. Drain on paper towels. Keep warm in oven on lowest setting and serve with hot Chinese mustard.

Serves 8 to 10.

Litchi Nut Fruit Dessert

2 cans (10 ounces) seedless litchi nuts, drained

4 cups fresh pineapple chunks

4 kiwi, peeled and thinly sliced

2 cups pitted Queen Anne cherries or white cherries

2 tablespoons Grand Marnier

Combine all the fruit in a large mixing bowl with the Grand Marnier. Spoon into 8 to 10 champagne glasses and chill before serving.

Serves 8 to 10.

St. Patrick's Day

Ireland, with its rolling hills and eternally green landscape,
truly is the Emerald Isle. It's no wonder that the celebration of
St. Patrick's Day is so full of local color.

St. Patrick's Day, both here and in Ireland, is a joyous affair that's full of good fellowship and conviviality. It celebrates St. Patrick, although no one really knows for sure whether or not March 17 represents his birthday, date of death, or anything at all. In fact, very little is actually known about St. Patty, although legend has it that he died at the age of 120, as did Moses.

What is known is that at the age of sixteen, Patrick was captured by the Gaels and taken by boat to Ireland where he was sold as a slave. It is said that during this period he experienced a spiritual awakening and began having dreams and visions that he felt were divinely inspired. One of these dreams contained a message that he should try to escape. He made a successful attempt and traveled 200 miles to find the ship the dream had told him he could expect. Three days later he landed in Britain—or Brittany, the name isn't clear. After landfall, his crew was facing starvation, but St. Patrick prayed for rescue, and a herd of wild pigs appeared. The crew was saved.

In 431 A.D., some say, St. Patrick was a candidate for a vacancy on the Irish episcopate. But a "friend" who wanted the job for himself revealed a now-forgotten sin from St. Patrick's past that kept him from getting the position. His lack of formal education didn't help, either. Instead, St. Patrick was made a priest and then a bishop. He went to Ireland and there he spent the rest of his life.

During the time of St. Patrick, Ireland was ruled primarily by a group of people called the Druids. The stories of some of St. Patrick's exploits are riddled with tales about his troubles with the Druids, who used fearful tactics to keep the Irish under their control. St. Patrick was hailed for his ability to throw off Druid domination and bring civilization and Christianity to Ireland.

In Ireland, St. Patrick's Day is not celebrated as elaborately as in the United States. The local inns produce a "Patrick Pot" of beer and whiskey, with bread and fish to go with it. And at breakfast tables in some homes, a plate of shamrocks is placed in front of the "master" of the house, who drowns the shamrocks in whiskey and sends the remainder of the newly opened bottle to the servants. In the evening, if you're lucky enough to be in Dublin, there's usually a ball held at St. Patrick's Hall in Dublin Castle.

In the United States, St. Patrick's Day is not just celebrated by the Irish. It has become everyone's holiday. Green clothing is donned by anyone who wants to partake of the festive spirit. Beer flows freely, even though, in fact, St. Patrick and his followers were abstinent.

In America, the first secular celebration of St. Patrick's Day appears to have been held in 1737 by the Charitable Irish Society of Boston, an organization that was founded for people of Irish heritage who were poor or infirm.

Actual parading started as an act of defiance against such groups as the Ku Klux Klan and others like it who didn't care for the Irish. The Irish got together and paraded in the streets to show their numbers and their pride. Today the largest parade can be found in New York City.

Through the centuries, the Irish diet has had very little meat. Although even the poorest people owned a cow or, at the very least, a goat, no animals were killed for food unless there had been a poor harvest.

Depending on their proximity to the sea or rivers and lakes, however, there seems to have been a lot of fish in the Irish diet. Grains, roots (both wild and cultivated), weeds, mushrooms, leeks, watercress, nettles, apples, nuts, and whortleberries —a European variety of blueberry—were all part of their food repertoire.

Potatoes, which became a staple of the Irish diet, came to Europe from Peru. They were hailed at first as an aphrodisiac. An old saying quoted by Malachi McCormick in *Irish Country Cooking* is, "Being boiled, baked, or roasted, eaten with good butter and salt...they increase seed and provoke lust, causing fruitfulness in both sexes."

And, contrary to popular thought, the national dish of Ireland is not corned beef and cabbage. It's a dish called colcannon, regionally known as cally or poundy. This is a dish made with boiled potatoes, cabbage, leeks, onions, wild garlic, and buttermilk. The whole thing is cooked in a three-legged pot called a bastable.

Here is the recipe—plus a few others— for a very special St. Patrick's Day dinner.

▲▲▲▲▲▲▲▲▲▲▲▲▲▲▲▲▲▲▲▲▲▲

St. Patrick's Day

M E N U

Colcannon • Irish Soda Bread

Mulled Claret • Irish Stew

Making use of local ingredients is very much a part of classic

Irish cuisine. In this case, potatoes and cabbage are combined to

create the national dish of Ireland: colcannon.

Served with some mulled claret, this is a meal in itself.

Colcannon

1 1-pound white cabbage, cored

1 teaspoon salt

**2 pounds potatoes, sliced into ¹/₄-inch slices
and boiled until tender**

**3 to 4 large leeks, thoroughly washed and
thinly sliced**

1¹/₂ cups half-and-half

¹/₂ teaspoon ground mace

Salt (to taste)

Freshly ground black pepper (to taste)

3 large cloves garlic, crushed

4 tablespoons sweet butter

In a large saucepan, bring 3 quarts of water to a boil over high heat. Add cabbage to the boiling water. Cook until tender, about 12 to 15 minutes. Drain off the water, allow the cabbage to cool slightly, and chop it roughly.

In another pot, cook the potatoes until tender, then drain and reserve. Place leeks in a saucepan. Cover with the half-and-half, then add mace, salt, pepper, and garlic. Over medium heat bring the leeks and half-and-half close to boiling, then turn the heat down to low and simmer 10 to 15 minutes or until the leeks are tender. Remove from heat and reserve.

Mash the potatoes well, by hand or using a ricer. Add the leek mixture and blend in with the potatoes, taking care not to break up the leeks too much. Next mash in the cabbage and finish with the butter, mixing until it is completely melted. Transfer to a 2-quart, ovenproof casserole and place under the broiler until golden brown, about 3 minutes.

Serves 6.

What Irish meal would be complete
without the inclusion of Irish soda bread?
While the classic recipe is given here,
try adding a tablespoon or two of fresh
chopped rosemary for an added treat.
The contrast of savory and sweet is worth
the experiment.

Irish Soda Bread

4 cups all-purpose flour

1 teaspoon baking soda

1 teaspoon cream of tartar

1 teaspoon salt

³/₄ cup granulated sugar

1 stick sweet butter, melted

¹/₂ cup seedless dark raisins

1¹/₄ cups plus 2 tablespoons buttermilk

Preheat oven to 350°F. Sift the dry ingredients into a large mixing bowl. Add the butter, raisins, and buttermilk. Mix until well blended. If the dough is too sticky to handle, dust with more flour. Turn the dough out onto a lightly floured surface and knead for 3 to 5 minutes, or until firm. Split the dough in half and shape into two loaves. Put the loaves on a buttered and floured baking sheet. Brush the loaves with buttermilk and dust with flour. Score the top of each loaf with an "X." Bake until golden brown, about 1 hour. Cool completely on a wire rack.

Makes 2 loaves.

Mulled Claret

1 large lemon, peeled and cut into 6 thin slices (remove pith and reserve both peel and pith)

6 cloves

¹/₂ teaspoon fresh nutmeg, grated

¹/₂ cup water

1 bottle claret (750 milliliters)

2 cups port

¹/₂ cup granulated sugar

In a 2-quart saucepan, simmer the lemon peel, pith, spices, and water for 20 minutes over medium-high heat. Add claret, port, and sugar. Heat the mixture thoroughly, but do not boil. Serve with peeled lemon slices.

Makes 6 cups.

Irish Stew

3 pounds stewing lamb, cut into 2-inch cubes

3 pounds new potatoes, thinly sliced

1 teaspoon salt (or to taste)

¹/₄ teaspoon freshly ground black pepper (or to taste)

2 large onions, thinly sliced

1 tablespoon fresh thyme, chopped

2¹/₂ cups beef broth or stock

¹/₄ cup fresh parsley, chopped

In a large 12-inch skillet, sear the lamb cubes on all sides over high heat. Remove from heat and reserve. Line the bottom of an 8-quart saucepan with a layer of sliced potatoes. Season with thyme, salt, and pepper. Add a layer of onion and season with more salt and pepper; then add a layer of lamb. Continue this process until all of the ingredients are used. Pour the stock over all. Bring to a boil over high heat. Reduce the heat to low and simmer, covered, about 1¹/₂ to 2 hours or until the lamb is tender. Sprinkle with fresh parsley.

Serves 6.

A Swedish Christmas

In Sweden, the long, cold Northern winters are truly enhanced

by the celebration of Christmas. The monotony of these winter

months is broken by the elaborate attention that the Christmas

season receives, and it is without a doubt a joyous time of year.

the Swedes both in their native land and in America are almost as well-known for their elaborate Christmas decorations as for their food. During long, cold Northern winters, the Christmas holidays are truly a high point. They reduce the monotony of the long winter months and bring joy into everyone's lives. On Swedish farms and even in the towns, during the romantic period of the nineteenth century, the walls of most homes were decorated with homemade textiles, wall hangings, and tapestries. Both timbered walls and whitewashed surfaces were covered with these brightly covered cloths—reflecting, perhaps, a cultural memory of churches in the Middle Ages.

The Swedes are heavy meat-eaters and this is reflected in their traditional Christmas fare. The Christmas pork sausage, for example, is one of the most important elements of Christmas dinner. Only the best-quality pork is used (both the lean and the fat). The filler, or binder, is gener-

ally potato flour. Ideally, the sausage is thinned with pork stock, not the milk that some modern cooks have begun to utilize. The sausage is then cooked in the stock from the Christmas hen. This sausage is thought by many to have a more distinct flavor than ordinary sausage. After the sausages are made, they are hung from a wooden sling under the kitchen rafters. They keep this way for months.

The centerpiece of many a Swedish Christmas table is a pig's head. It can be purchased already cured so that all you need do is poach it. If you want to stick the classic apple in its mouth, insert a large enough object that is impervious to heat in the mouth while poaching to set it open. After poaching, wipe off the fat with a towel that has been soaked in white vinegar. The vinegar helps to remove the fat so the garnishes will adhere. The pig's head must be cooked until it becomes tender, or until the meat comes away from the bone but still retains its shape on the

head. Traditionally, the head is decorated with green cabbage and colored tissue paper, which can be inserted in the ears.

Another important part of a Swedish Christmas dinner is the herring salad called salmagundi, which is a dish deeply rooted in ancient traditions. Oddly enough, the herring is occasionally now omitted from the recipe, although herring—flavored with coriander—is sometimes found on the Christmas table.

Brawn, another traditional element of the Christmas table, must be included here. Brawn is a liquid extracted from veal and pork. While it can be purchased at specialty stores, it is never as good as homemade. The old version was made from the pig's head, shoulder, and rind, but since there is so much concern these days with dietary fat, this older version has been replaced by a leaner variety.

The Christmas ham is the most substantial dish of the Swedish repast. It is first boiled, then broiled or grilled, and finally decorated with a ruff cut out of colored papers. It is accompanied by mustard, red cabbage, and brussels sprouts.

The healthiest dish at a Swedish Christmas dinner is the *lutfisk,* a sun-dried and lime-cured fish. In days gone by, the fish was cut into pieces and put into a lime cure on the ninth day of December, then removed on Christmas Eve. The best way to serve *lutfisk,* according to many Swedes, is as a pudding, accompanied by butter and béchamel sauce.

The Christmas rice pudding is perhaps the most well-known of all Christmas dishes, although lately it has fallen slightly out of favor since the Swedish Christmas dinner is altogether a very heavy affair. After eating a smorgasbord of pork, followed by *lutfisk,* and a vast array of puff pastries, breads, and almond cakes with jam, the rice pudding is just a touch too much for many Swedes.

Most Swedes, however, do leave room for the boiled bread twists called *kringlor.* After being rolled out, they are boiled in water, then removed to a baking sheet and finished in the oven. They are usually made in two shapes: a double-entwined circle, and an oval shape with two ends of the dough attached. These ends are then notched with a knife to form "fingers."

Here are the blueprints for your own Swedish feast.

▲▲▲▲▲▲▲▲▲▲▲▲▲▲▲▲▲▲▲▲▲▲▲

A Swedish Christmas

M E N U

Gravlax with Dill · Pork Brawn

Herring and Potato Casserole

Christmas Baked Ham

Vegetables au Gratin

Although salmon is found in abundance in the North, the Swedes

still honor the fish with special attention during its preparation.

This gravlax (above) is a salt-and-dill-cured salmon, which has

been allowed to marinate for several days.

Gravlax with Dill

3 tablespoons coarse salt

2 tablespoons sugar

1 tablespoon freshly ground white pepper

3 pounds salmon fillets, with skin on

1 tablespoon vegetable oil

2 tablespoons cognac

1 large bunch fresh dill, finely chopped

In a small bowl, combine salt, sugar, and pepper. Rub the salmon with oil and cognac, then season with half of the sugar, salt, and pepper mixtures.

Spread half of the dill in a shallow baking dish. Place the salmon on top of the dill, skin-side down. Cover with remaining dill. Cover the salmon with plastic wrap, then a double thickness of aluminum foil. Place a heavy pot or several plates on top to weigh it down. Refrigerate 3 to 7 days, turning and basting the fish every 12 hours.

Slice the cured salmon in long thin strips and serve with Dill Sauce (recipe follows), lemon wedges, and black bread. *Serves 10 to 12.*

Dill Sauce:

3 tablespoons grain mustard

1 tablespoon sugar

2 tablespoons white wine vinegar

$^1/_2$ cup safflower oil

$^1/_2$ cup fresh dill, chopped

Salt and pepper to taste

In a small bowl, combine mustard, sugar, and vinegar. Using a wire whisk, add the oil slowly in a thin stream until well emulsified. Add dill, salt, and pepper.

Makes $^3/_4$ cup.

Pork Brawn

2¼ quarts cold water

2 pounds split pig's feet

½ pound pork shoulder

½ pound chicken necks, skin removed

1 small onion, peeled and quartered

1 small carrot, cut into 1-inch pieces

8 black peppercorns

2 teaspoons kosher salt

1 bay leaf

10 large cloves garlic

Salt (to taste)

½ teaspoon freshly ground black pepper (or to taste)

3 hard-boiled eggs

In a 6-quart stockpot, combine water, pig's feet, pork shoulder, and chicken necks. Bring to a boil over high heat. Reduce to a simmer, skimming the foam as it rises to the top. Add the onion, carrot, peppercorns, and salt. Partially cover the pot and cook the stock over a very low heat for 4 to 5 hours or until the broth is very rich and reduced by half. One hour before broth is ready, add the bay leaf.

After the stock is cooked, strain the liquid through several layers of cheesecloth into a clean pot. There should be about 1 quart. Discard the carrot, onion, and pig's feet. Remove the meat from the chicken necks and shred it along with the pork. Peel the garlic cloves and push them through a garlic press. Stir in salt and pepper and mix well with the shredded meats.

Prepare 2 1-quart molds by brushing them very lightly with vegetable oil. Pour enough broth to cover the bottom of the molds generously, then refrigerate until the broth has gelled. Top the gelled layer with slices of hard-boiled eggs. Place a layer of meat on top of the eggs and pour the remaining broth over them to cover. Refrigerate overnight. Scrape off any fat that has formed on the top.

To unmold, fill a large bowl with hot water. Carefully dip the mold into the hot water within 1 inch of its top for 30 seconds. Place a serving platter over the top of the mold and invert the brawn onto the platter. Slice and serve with spicy Russian mustard.

Serves 10.

Some of the ingredients found in this pork brawn might be

unfamiliar and dissuade you from trying this recipe. However, if

you allow your curiosity about other cultures and their food to get

the best of you, you'll be rewarded by the rich flavor of this Swedish specialty.

Herring and Potato Casserole

8 salt herring fillets

7 large potatoes, peeled and thinly sliced

2 large onions, thinly sliced

2 cloves garlic, minced

Freshly ground black pepper (to taste)

¹/₂ cup dry bread crumbs

¹/₄ cup butter

Preheat oven to 400°F. Soak the salt herring fillets overnight in cold water. Drain the fillets and pat dry; cut into bite-size pieces.

Arrange the herring, potatoes, and onions in alternating rows in an 8×8-inch well-buttered rectangular baking dish. Season with black pepper. Sprinkle the top with bread crumbs and dot with butter. Bake for 30 minutes, then turn down the oven to 300°F and continue baking until the potatoes are tender, about 20 minutes. *Serves 6 to 8.*

Christmas Baked Ham

1 8- to 10-pound smoked ham, precooked

4 bay leaves

6 whole cloves

6 peppercorns

4 cups Madeira wine

Cooked prunes and apple rings for garnish

Coating:

1 egg white

1 tablespoon dry mustard

¹/₄ cup brown sugar

1 cup dried, seasoned bread crumbs

Preheat oven to 350°F. Over high heat, add ham to a large stockpot and cover with boiling water. Add bay leaves, cloves, and peppercorns, and bring to a boil. Reduce temperature to medium and simmer until just tender, about 2¹/₂ hours. Drain, add wine, and simmer 30 minutes longer, basting ham thoroughly. Remove pot from heat and allow ham to cool slightly in wine broth. Remove cooled ham, reserving the wine broth. Strain this liquid through a double-thick piece of cheesecloth and reserve 2 cups. Skin the ham but leave a collar of skin around the shank bone. Place the ham in a baking dish.

Combine egg white, dry mustard, and brown sugar, and mix well. Coat the surface of the meat with the mixture, then pat on the bread crumbs. Bake 45 minutes.

To serve, transfer ham to a heated platter. Garnish with cooked prunes and apple rings. Serve sauce (recipe follows) on the side.

Serves 10 to 12.

Sauce:

¹/₄ cup butter

¹/₄ cup flour

2 cups reserved wine broth

2 cups beef broth

Salt and pepper (to taste)

Melt butter over high heat, blend in flour, and cook 1 to 2 minutes, stirring constantly. Gradually stir in reserved wine broth and beef broth until desired consistency. Season with salt and pepper. *Makes 4 cups.*

Vegetables Au Gratin
(Gronsaksgratin)

4 tablespoons butter

3 tablespoons flour

1¹/₂ cups heavy cream

1¹/₂ cups chicken broth

3 egg yolks

Salt and pepper (to taste)

2 cups cauliflower florets, blanched

2 cups carrots, peeled, sliced, and blanched

4 cups cooked peas

4 sliced tomatoes

4 ounces Emmenthaler cheese, grated

Preheat oven to 400°F. In a small saucepan, melt butter over high heat. Stirring constantly with a wooden spoon, add the flour all at once and cook 1 to 2 minutes. Gradually beat in the cream and chicken broth. Stir over low heat for 10 minutes until it starts to thicken. Keep hot.

In a medium-size mixing bowl, beat the egg yolks well. Slowly beat a few tablespoons of the hot sauce into the yolks, then stir this mixture into the saucepan. Heat through but do not boil. Remove the saucepan from the heat and season with salt and pepper.

Layer the cauliflower, carrots, and peas in a well-buttered baking dish. Pour in the sauce. Layer on the tomato slices. Season with more salt and pepper and top with grated cheese. Bake until cheese is melted, about 10 minutes, then brown under the broiler.

Serves 6 to 8.

The Festival Of San Gennaro

*The crowds can be thick, but the atmosphere is always friendly
at the Festival of San Gennaro in New York City's Little Italy.
At nighttime, the lights from the surrounding vendors flood the
sky, but perhaps most memorable are the wonderful aromas
that fill the air.*

*a*mericans with roots in Italy have played a very important role in the history of New York City as well as other parts of North America. Quite a few Italian-Americans were part of the group who settled in Dutch New Amsterdam, and a small group of Italian-Protestants were thought to have settled in Stony Brook, Staten Island, in 1657. Moreover, during the early part of the nineteenth century, many Italians found New York a refuge from political turmoil. By 1880, there were almost 12,000 Italians living in the city.

The mass exodus of Italians from their native Italy occurred mainly between the years 1880 and 1910, when outbreaks of malaria and cholera were of epidemic proportions. Along with disease there was severe poverty. At the same time, America was undergoing rapid industrial expansion, and the need for large numbers of unskilled laborers was immense, so many Italians saw hope in the new world.

The majority of these Italian immigrants came from the southern and central regions of the country, such as Sicily, Abruzzi, Calabria, and Apulia. Over 80 percent were men who left their families behind in Italy. They took what money they made in the United States and sent the largest portion back to their families. And since there was still such a deep connection to their homeland, these men often would take only seasonal jobs—at the end of which they would return to their Italian cities and villages.

But gradually families united in New York City, especially toward the lower part of Mulberry Street, which is now right in the heart of Chinatown. "Little Italy," as it was called, reached as far north as Houston Street, and east and west from the Bowery to Broadway. This area degenerated into a slum that was torn down eventually and replaced by Columbus Park, and today the southern border of Little Italy has moved back toward Canal Street.

World War I and the quota system slowed the flow of immigrants after 1910. But the Italian-American population in New York City is still high—an estimated two million—with the majority descended from southern Italians. There are even reports of areas in the city populated only by members of the same Italian village. It's as if some of the villages had moved as a whole. This type of unity appears to give Italian neighborhoods the solid foundation on which they maintain their culture.

As the oldest Italian quarter of New York, Little Italy also happens to be one of the largest tourist attractions as well. There is a wonderful neighborhood feeling that exists here, which makes this part of New York unique. At night, especially during the spring and summer months, the cafés expand onto the sidewalks. People stroll casually along, periodically stopping to talk—not infrequently in Italian. Still others seat themselves on folding chairs outside their apartments to watch the daily activities. Women hang out their windows leaning on pillows—which appear to be permanent fixtures on their sills—to check out the neighborhood goings-on. And shopkeepers address you on a first-name basis, as if you were a member of their extended family.

Over the years, Little Italy has undergone a significant overhaul of its general appearance. Most of the six-story brownstone walk-ups that existed for over a century still remain, but many of the street-level restaurants and shops have been modernized. Fortunately, much of the area's original charm has been preserved. But even though a fresh face has been put on Little Italy, the number of Italian-Americans who occupy these buildings is steadily decreasing. And it has, of late, become a chic place to live.

One of the reasons, no doubt, is the famous San Gennaro festival, which is held for eleven days in mid-September. Many New Yorkers as well as out-of-towners flock to the neighborhood. It's truly a sight to behold. Colored neon lights illuminate the streets, which are filled with people engaged in games of chance or eating from one of the seemingly hundreds of food wagons selling calzone, pizza, zeppole, and *gelate*. The smells of sausage and peppers permeate the air.

Descendants of relatives who came from Naples more than a century ago honor their patron saint, San Gennaro—also known as Januarius—each year at this time with solemn masses, religious processions, games, and a wealth of traditional Neapolitan food, which abounds everywhere you turn. It's a time for letting out all the stops and celebrating to the fullest. And it's such a deeply rooted part of New York that September in the city wouldn't be the same without it.

One of the traditional food favorites to be sampled is called calzone, which translated means "pants." It's a deep-fried turnover made from pizza dough and stuffed with any imaginable filling that the cook dreams up. Another favorite is a sandwich with either spicy or sweet sausage sautéed with red and green peppers and onions, served on a hunk of Italian bread. It's delicious and should be tried at least once.

For dessert, save room for zeppole, a deep-fried doughnut without the hole that's covered in powdered sugar. Ice creams (*gelate*), ices, and Italian pastries are found all over the area.

If you can't wait until next year's festival for a taste, try whipping up one or two of the following recipes.

▲▲▲▲▲▲▲▲▲▲▲▲▲▲▲▲▲▲▲▲▲▲

The Festival of San Gennaro

M E N U

Mini Pizzas · Calzone

Hot Sausage and Pepper Heros

Zeppole

Mini Pizzas

1 package active dry yeast

1 teaspoon sugar

1 cup warm water

2¹/₂ cups all-purpose flour

¹/₂ teaspoon salt

2 tablespoons olive oil

2 chopped onions

2 cloves garlic, crushed

4 to 6 plum tomatoes, peeled and sliced

1 tablespoon tomato paste

Salt and pepper (to taste)

¹/₄ pound pepperoni, cut into small pieces

4 ounces mozzarella cheese, shredded

24 oil-cured olives, pitted and sliced

Preheat oven to 450°F. In a large bowl, dissolve yeast and sugar with ¹/₂ cup warm water. Let stand about 5 minutes or until bubbly. In the meantime, in a separate bowl sift flour and salt together. Stir in the yeast mixture and remaining ¹/₂ cup water. Combine ingredients with a wooden spoon until a ball is formed.

Terrific for serving at cocktail parties, these mini pizzas may not be traditional food in Italy, but there is no mistaking that in the United States, pizza is most definitely Italian.

Turn out onto a well-floured board and knead at least 5 minutes or until smooth and elastic. Place dough in a greased bowl, cover, and let rise in a warm place for about an hour or until doubled in bulk.

In a large 12-inch skillet, heat olive oil over high heat. When hot, add onions and garlic. Cook, stirring, for 2 minutes. Stir in tomatoes and simmer uncovered, 15 to 20 minutes. Add tomato paste and season.

Punch dough down and turn out onto a floured board and knead lightly. Roll out to $1/2$ inch thickness and cut into 3-inch rounds. Arrange on greased baking sheets. Top with tomato sauce, pepperoni, cheese, and olives. Bake 20 to 30 minutes. *Makes 12 individual pizzas.*

Calzone

1 package active dry yeast

1 cup lukewarm water (about 115°F)

1 teaspoon sugar

1 teaspoon salt

1 tablespoon extra-virgin olive oil

2$1/2$ to 3 cups flour

$1/4$ pound fresh mozzarella, coarsely grated or shredded

$1/2$ pound ricotta cheese

8 thin slices prosciutto

1 quart vegetable oil for frying

In a large mixing bowl, combine yeast, water, and sugar. Stir until the yeast is dissolved. Set in a warm place for 5 minutes or until foamy. Add the salt and the olive oil, and mix well. Slowly add enough flour to make the dough barely firm enough to handle. Knead the dough on a lightly floured board until smooth and elastic. Divide the dough into 8 equal parts. Shape into balls and place on 2 oiled pans so there are at least 4 inches between each ball. Flatten slightly, cover, and allow to rise in a warm place for 1 hour or until doubled in bulk.

While the dough is rising, combine the mozzarella with the ricotta cheese in a small bowl. Cover and set aside.

When the dough has risen, place balls of dough on a floured surface and flatten each into 6- to 7-inch circles. Place a slice of prosciutto on each circle and place $1/8$ of cheese mixture on each. Fold ham neatly around the cheese, encasing it completely. Fold the dough over the filling in turnover fashion and pinch the edges together to seal well.

In a heavy-gauge pot or deep-fat fryer, heat oil to 350°F (measure with a deep-fat-fry thermometer). Slowly add 1 or 2 calzones at a time to the hot oil, turning until nicely browned on both sides. Drain on a paper towel and serve hot. *Serves 8.*

Hot Sausage and Pepper Heros

2 pounds hot Italian sausage

1 large onion, thinly sliced

3 large cloves garlic, crushed

1 teaspoon oregano

Salt and pepper (to taste)

2 red bell peppers, cut into thin strips

2 green bell peppers, cut into thin strips

2 yellow peppers, cut into thin strips

8 6-inch wedges of Italian bread

In a large skillet over high heat, sauté the sausage 5 to 7 minutes or until nicely browned on all sides and cooked through. Remove sausages and drain on paper towels. Add onion to skillet. Cook 3 to 5 minutes until wilted and lightly browned. Add garlic, oregano, salt, and pepper. Add peppers, reduce heat to medium, and cook, stirring, for 5 minutes. Cover and continue cooking for 15 minutes longer, stirring occasionally, until the vegetables are soft but not mushy. Slice the bread wedges horizontally without cutting all the way through. Fill each sandwich with sausages and spread some of the pepper and onion mixture over the top. Serve hot.

Makes 8 sandwiches.

Zeppole

2 cups all-purpose flour

$1/4$ teaspoon salt

1 tablespoon baking powder

$1/2$ teaspoon ground mace

2 large eggs

$1/3$ cup granulated sugar

$1/2$ cup milk

1 quart vegetable oil for frying

Confectioner's sugar

Make certain that all the ingredients are at room temperature. Sift the flour, salt, baking powder, and mace into a medium-size bowl. In a separate bowl, beat the eggs lightly, add the sugar, and continue beating until the mixture is lemony yellow. Stir in the milk. Pour egg mixture into the flour and mix well with a wooden spoon. Cover with plastic wrap and allow this to stand at room temperature for 30 minutes.

Heat the vegetable oil in a large heavy-gauge pot or deep-fryer until the temperature is 375°F (measured with a deep-fat-fry thermometer) or until a 1-inch cube of white bread browns in 1 minute. Drop the batter by the tablespoon into the hot oil, cooking as many as 3 to 4 at a time. Fry them for 3 minutes or until golden brown. Remove with a slotted spoon or small strainer and drain on a paper towel. Sprinkle or dunk in a bag of confectioner's sugar. These are great hot or cold.

Serves 8.

If you've ever wondered what was so special about fried dough,

try a zeppole. These powdered sugar treats are a delight to the

palate.

A Greek Easter

Greek Easter is the most important and festive of all religious
Greek holidays both in Greece and in Greek-American
communities across the United States.

Reflecting the ancient dominance of the Greek Orthodox Church in the lives of its members, Easter is celebrated as the pinnacle of the Greek festival year, both in Greece and in Greek-American communities throughout the United States.

In days past, Easter—or Carnival, as it was sometimes called—took place over a three-week period. It began with the firing of guns or the beating of drums by a town crier. After this came "Meat Week," during which time a pig was slaughtered and consumed, followed by "Cheese Week," when only cheese, milk, and eggs were eaten. The forty days of Lent that followed Cheese Week were meant for fasting, and no gaiety could be displayed. There were no dances, weddings, or fairs, and women put their jewelry away since any type of adornment was deemed disrespectful. It was truly a somber period.

A common belief among the Greeks was that during the first week of Carnival the souls of the dead were freed from bondage and allowed to walk among the living. Accordingly, the first bite of food and drink of wine taken at the Carnival meal were accompanied by the prayer, "May God forgive the souls of the dead."

The principal days consecrated to the dead were Meat Week Saturday, Cheese Week Saturday, and the first Saturday of Lent. Each of the three was called "All Souls' Day." A group of housewives prepared a special dish, which was distributed to neighbors so the souls of the dead relatives might be forgiven, and on All Souls' Day, a long procession of black-garbed women and girls made their way to the cemetery carrying dishes of *kollyva,* decorated with powdered sugar, cinnamon, walnuts, sesame seeds, pomegranate, parsley, and currants. These offerings were placed on ancestral graves while candles were lit and incense was burned.

In some areas of Greece, the feast on the Sunday evening of Cheese Week was for the whole village. The mayor would set his table and invite everyone to dinner. Foods that were traditionally served included macaroni, eggs, cheese pies, milk pies, and a special dish called *tyrozoumi,* a cheese broth.

In some cases *tyrozoumi* was placed on the table first. There were often small games that people would play before consuming their soup, and certain sayings frequently accompanied the eating of the various foods as well. When the eggs were served as the last dish, for example, they would be accompanied by the saying, "With an egg I close my mouth, with an egg I shall open it again." This referred to the dyed red eggs, which symbolized the blood of Christ, used at the end of Lent.

The Greek Orthodox services for Easter actually began the Saturday before Easter Sunday and were recognized as preliminary to the Holy Resurrection. In the middle of what is known as the Divine Liturgy, the priest might have thrown some bay leaves throughout the church to represent the joy of the event about to occur—the resurrection of Christ.

After a church service celebrating the rising of Christ from the dead on Easter morning, each family carried home a lit candle and, on entering the house, paused to allow the smoke from the candle to form a cross near the top of the door frame. The long Lent fast was broken as the family consumed a traditional meal of *mageritsa,* a soup made from lamb organ meats and seasoned with scallions, dill, and *avgolemono* (lemon egg) sauce; *lambropsoma,* a Greek Easter bread; lamb; potatoes; and Easter eggs.

The eggs were cracked against each other by members of the family, who said "Christos Anesti!" ("Christ has risen!") and "Alithos Anesti!" ("Indeed He has risen!"). The egg itself was a symbol of the resurrection, since it contained a life form. The cracking of the egg symbolized the loosening of the bonds that held man captive for so long, and the fact that now, in Christ, man could be free. The greetings, "Christos Anesti" and "Alithos Anesti" took the place of "Good Morning" and "Good Evening."

Easter cake made with red eggs and sprinkled with sesame seeds, plus perhaps *kourabiedes,* a favorite shortbread cookie that appears at all festive occasions, would complete the meal.

Here are a few recipes to turn your Easter dinner into a Greek celebration.

▲▲▲▲▲▲▲▲▲▲▲▲▲▲▲▲▲▲▲▲▲

A Greek Easter

M E N U

Spanakopetes

Chicken Soup with Avgolemono Sauce

Roast Leg of Lamb with Garlic and
Fresh Oregano · Roasted Potatoes

Greek-style Braised Green Beans

Lambropsoma · Kourabiedes

Spanakopetes are little pies filled with spinach and feta cheese and folded into phyllo pastry sheets. This recipe includes a lower fat, lower salt farmer's cheese for a healthier variation.

Spanakopetes

¹/₄ cup extra-virgin olive oil

3 large cloves garlic, minced

1 medium onion, finely chopped

1 10¹/₂-ounce package frozen, chopped spinach, thawed and drained

¹/₂ pound feta cheese

¹/₂ pound farmer's cheese

2 eggs, beaten

¹/₄ to ¹/₂ cup dry bread crumbs

¹/₄ pound sweet butter

¹/₂ pound phyllo pastry sheets

Preheat oven to 425°F. In a large 12-inch skillet, heat oil over medium-high heat. When hot, sauté garlic and onions for 3 to 5 minutes. Add drained spinach. Reduce heat to low and simmer, stirring occasionally, until most of the moisture has evaporated. Remove from heat. Add feta cheese and farmer's cheese in small crumbled pieces; blend well. Add eggs and bread crumbs. Set aside. Melt butter. Carefully cut phyllo into 3 equal portions. Refrigerate ⅔ of the pastry until needed and cover the remaining ⅓ with a slightly damp towel.

Remove one sheet of phyllo pastry, place on a flat surface, and brush well with the melted butter. Fold in the long sides toward the middle, making a strip about 2 inches wide. Butter again. Place 1 tablespoon of spinach filling in the bottom right-hand corner of the strip and fold over into a triangle shape. Continue folding, making sure with each fold that the bottom edge is parallel with the alternate side edge. Lightly butter finished triangle. Continue in this manner until all the filling and phyllo sheets are used. Bake on sheet pans for 20 minutes or until golden brown. Allow to cool 5 minutes before serving.

Makes about 40 pieces.

Chicken Soup with Avgolemono Sauce

1 3⅓-pound stewing hen

½ teaspoon black peppercorns

1 large carrot, cut into 1-inch pieces

1 medium onion, cut into quarters

1 stalk celery, cut into 1-inch pieces

1½ teaspoons salt

1 cup white rice

In an 8-quart pot fitted with a lid, add hen and enough cold water to cover. Bring to a boil over high heat. Reduce heat to medium and add peppercorns, carrot, onion, and celery. Cover and simmer 2 to 4 hours or until hen is tender. Strain broth and remove extra fat. Reserve hen for another use. Add rice to broth and continue to cook until tender, about 10 to 15 minutes. Remove from heat. When boiling subsides, combine with Avgolemono Sauce (recipe follows).

Makes 8 to 10 servings.

Avgolemono Sauce

4 large eggs, separated

Juice of two lemons

Beat egg whites until stiff peaks form. Add yolks one at a time and continue beating. Gradually beat in lemon juice. Add a small amount of hot broth to the egg sauce to temper it, then combine this with the rest of the broth. Return to medium heat and stir constantly and rapidly until soup starts to thicken. Do not boil.

Makes ¼ cup.

Roast Leg of Lamb with Garlic and Fresh Oregano

1 7-pound leg of lamb

7 to 10 large garlic cloves, peeled and thinly sliced

$^1/_2$ cup extra-virgin olive oil

$^1/_2$ cup fresh oregano, chopped

2 teaspoons salt

1 tablespoon cracked black pepper

Preheat oven to 450°F. With a paring knife, make small incisions in the lamb and insert garlic slivers evenly throughout. Combine olive oil, oregano, salt, and pepper. Rub over entire leg of lamb. Set lamb on a roasting rack in a large roasting pan. Cook for about 30 minutes. Reduce heat to 350°F and continue cooking for about 3$^1/_2$ hours, or until the internal temperature reaches 155° to 160°F on a meat thermometer.

Serves 8 to 10.

Roasted Potatoes

2 pounds all-purpose potatoes, peeled and quartered

2 tablespoons olive oil

$1/2$ cup oil-cured olives, pitted and chopped

2 tablespoons capers in balsamic vinegar

2 tablespoons fresh parsley, chopped

Salt and freshly ground pepper (to taste)

Place potatoes in lamb-roasting pan 45 minutes to 1 hour before lamb is done. Cook until tender and golden brown, which may require some basting. When done, remove from pan, drain on paper towels, and keep warm in the oven.

Meanwhile, in an 8-inch sauté pan, heat oil over medium-high heat. When hot, sauté olives and capers together for 1 to 2 minutes. Add potatoes to pan and toss to coat. Sprinkle with parsley and season with salt and pepper.

Serves 8 to 10.

Greek-Style Braised String Beans

2 tablespoons extra-virgin olive oil

1 medium onion, finely chopped

2 large cloves garlic, minced

1 tablespoon tomato paste

1 13 $1/2$-ounce can chicken broth

2 large tomatoes, peeled, seeded, and chopped

2 pounds string beans

$1/4$ cup fresh mint, chopped

Salt and freshly ground pepper (to taste)

In a 12-inch skillet, heat oil over high heat. When hot, add onion, stirring constantly 1 to 2 minutes or until transparent. Add garlic and continue cooking 30 seconds longer. Stir in tomato paste, broth, and tomatoes. Bring to a boil. Reduce heat to low and simmer 2 to 3 minutes. Add string beans, and cook, stirring occasionally, for 2 to 3 minutes or until tender. Sprinkle with fresh mint and season with salt and pepper.

Serves 6 to 8.

Lambropsoma
(Greek Easter Bread)

¹/₂ cup lukewarm water

2 packages active dry yeast

¹/₂ cup milk

¹/₄ pound sweet butter, melted and cooled

*5 cups and 1 cup to adjust while kneading
all-purpose flour*

3 eggs, beaten

¹/₄ cup plus 1 teaspoon sugar

¹/₄ teaspoon salt

¹/₂ teaspoon anise flavoring

5 hard-boiled eggs, dyed red

Egg wash (egg beaten with water)

3 tablespoons sesame seeds

Preheat oven to 350°F. In a medium-size mixing bowl, add lukewarm water and 1 teaspoon sugar to yeast; combine until bubbly. Stir in milk. In a large mixing bowl, blend butter with 5 cups flour and stir in eggs, remaining sugar, salt, and anise flavoring. Add yeast mixture and blend thoroughly. Turn out dough onto a lightly floured board and knead for 10 minutes or until dough is smooth and elastic. Put into a greased bowl, cover with a kitchen towel, and let rise in a warm place for about 2 hours or until doubled in bulk.

   Punch down dough and knead again until smooth. Form dough into a loaf. Place loaf into a large floured bread pan and make five depressions in it: one in the center and the others in the four opposite edges of the loaf. Place eggs in these depressions. Cover pan with towel again and allow dough to rise 1¹/₂ hours longer or until doubled in bulk. Brush with egg wash and sprinkle with sesame seeds. Bake for about 45 minutes or until golden brown.

Makes 1 loaf.

Kourabiedes

1 pound sweet butter, at room temperature

¹/₂ cup confectioner's sugar

2 egg yolks, lightly beaten

¹/₂ cup blanched almonds, finely chopped

2 ounces brandy

¹/₄ cup orange juice

2 teaspoons grated orange rind

1 teaspoon baking powder

5 cups sifted flour

Preheat oven to 400°F. Using an electric mixer, cream the butter until very light in a large bowl. Beat in sugar, egg yolks, almonds, brandy, orange juice, and grated rind. Sift baking powder with flour and slowly blend into butter-sugar mixture. Shape into small crescent shapes and place on unbuttered baking sheets. Bake for about 20 minutes or until golden. Sift powdered sugar over all the cookies when they are removed from the oven. Cool thoroughly before storing. These may be frozen.

Makes approximately 10 dozen small cookies.

Lambropsoma, or Greek Easter bread, is baked with eggs, which can be dyed red to symbolize the blood of Christ and the resurrection.

The Iroquois Green Corn Festival

*The Iroquois Green Corn Festival on the Onondaga Indian
Reservation in upstate New York is celebrated at the end of
August. The Onondagas are just one of five Iroquois nations who
still celebrate this festival.*

*t*he Iroquois Green Corn Festival is usually held near the end of August at the Onondaga Indian Reservation in upstate New York. The Onondagas who sponsor it are one of five Iroquois nations still in existence that celebrate the festival. The other tribes are the Cayuga, Seneca, Oneida, and Mohawk.

Like many of the festivals the Iroquois celebrate, the Green Corn Festival is one of thanksgiving. Those long and laborious hours devoted to planting and nurturing the corn crop have been completed and the corn is almost ready to pick. The workers' thanks are expressed through dances, songs, games, and food—all of which possess a religious and deeply spiritual significance. Long ago, the Green Corn Festival was also a time when scattered peoples would come together for socializing prior to heading out for the fall camps.

There are many Native American legends explaining how corn came to the land. The Iroquois tribes of New York State, for example, tell the story of a spirit woman who walked across the fields with corn and pumpkins sprouting from her footprints.

The origin of most Native American foods is not really known, although through the extensive research of both anthropologists and botanists it appears that most of these foods came from the pre-Inca cultures of Peru. It is almost a certainty that corn originated there, for the earliest motifs of maize—its stalks, ears, and tassles—were found in the country's archaeological sites.

The miracle of corn is its utter helplessness. Because it cannot reproduce itself when cast as seed, each kernel must be set carefully in the soil to grow. Some scientists now believe that corn, even that known to early Native Americans, was actually a hybrid of two wild grasses, neither of which can reproduce easily.

The Native Americans' respect for corn is not surprising since it was a source of life. And given its importance, it is also not surprising that the Native Americans held a joyous celebration each summer when the ears of corn were ripe.

The Green Corn Festival in Onondaga, for example, takes place on the third weekend in August. Preparations start weeks before. Historically at least, every woman would clean house and get rid of old clothing and old dishes before the festival—a kind of "out with the old and in with the new." The men purged their bodies with a strong emetic known as the "black drink," a beverage that was brewed from *yaupon* leaves (a plant related to holly).

When every village was thoroughly cleaned, the ceremony would begin with the lighting of a new fire on the village altar. It was a time of great rejoicing for all involved. The repast that the Native Americans enjoyed often included such succulent foods as spit-roasted game birds and sweet yams baked in hot ashes. Ears of corn were roasted in the husk or the young, juicy kernels were made into puddings or cakes. The Iroquois picked tart, wild cherries and simmered them along with maple sugar. They prepared an applesauce made extra-rich by the inclusion of apple skins. They smoked eel for savory stews. They also stuffed wild ducks with apples and grapes, then turned them slowly over crackling flames so that the skin was crispy and the meat moist.

Corn soup was also featured, and it is usually the main dish served at the modern Green Corn Festival. There are numerous interpretations of this soup that change from tribe to tribe and cook to cook. Basically, however, the soup contains corn or white hominy, meat (usually pork), beans, and vegetables such as squash and turnips.

The classical accompaniment to this festival dish is Ghost Bread. Its name is derived from its use in ceremonies for the dead. It is also slightly ghostlike in appearance, since it doesn't brown during baking. It can be baked in a variety of ways and shapes, depending on the creative nature of the cook. Corn bread is another specialty that can be eaten at the festival, as is corn on the cob, sassafras tea, and venison, which is served in the form of venison burgers. This latter item is a recent addition to the feast.

As a public exhibition, the Green Corn Festival has been in existence since 1930 and was brought about with the help of Chief David Hill. Today it serves as a fundraising event for the volunteer fire department of the Onondaga Reservation. Not only are native foods sold at the festival but a vast array of beautiful Indian handi-

crafts can also be purchased—beaded necklaces, earrings, bracelets, carved wooden pipes, soapstone carvings, and a few Native American paintings produced by local artists. Both men and women participate in the traditional dances, which are performed in traditional dress and accompanied by at least two or three singers.

Some of the native foods you might have the opportunity to sample are cakes or puddings made with tender young kernels of corn, or wild cherries simmered in maple sugar, or perhaps an extra-flavorful and rich applesauce. You might also sample hearty stews made with smoked eel or wild ducks that have been stuffed with apples and grapes and slowly roasted over an open fire.

Here are a few recipes to give you a taste of what's in store.

▲▲▲▲▲▲▲▲▲▲▲▲▲▲▲▲▲▲▲

The Iroquois Green Corn Festival

M E N U

Marinated Venison Burgers

Ghost Bread · Iroquois Corn Soup

Smoked Eel Stew

Iroquoian Wild Lettuce Salad

With Vinaigrette Dressing

Corn Pudding

Because venison is leaner than chicken—and has tremendous

flavor—it makes a tasty and healthy addition to any gathering.

Marinated Venison Burgers

2 cups red wine

5 to 6 cloves garlic, crushed

¹/₂ cup chopped onion

2 tablespoons Dijon-style mustard

1 tablespoon green peppercorns in brine, drained and chopped

2 tablespoons coarse sea salt

1 whole bay leaf

2 pounds venison

1 pound Italian sausage meat (Ask your butcher to grind the two meats together.)

In a 2-quart saucepan, combine red wine, garlic, onion, mustard, peppercorns, salt, and bay leaf over high heat. Bring to a boil. Reduce heat to low and simmer 2 to 3 minutes. Remove from heat and allow it to cool completely.

Combine venison with sausage meat, if your butcher hasn't already done so, and mix thoroughly. Make 6 8-ounce patties and place them in a shallow glass or ceramic dish large enough to hold them in one layer. When the marinade is completely cooled, pour over venison burgers. Cover with plastic wrap and refrigerate one to two days, turning periodically during that time.

Preheat broiler, or better yet, prepare a charcoal grill. Drain the marinade and cook 7 to 10 minutes on each side, or until meat is no longer pink. Remove to a serving platter and keep warm until ready to serve. Serve with Ghost Bread (recipe follows).
Serves 6.

Ghost Bread

4 cups all-purpose flour

¹/₂ teaspoon salt

4 teaspoons baking powder

¹/₄ cup vegetable shortening or lard

1 cup low-fat milk

Preheat oven to 375°F. Combine flour, salt, and baking powder in a large mixing bowl. Cut in the shortening with a pastry blender until the mixture resembles coarse oatmeal. Add the milk gradually, stirring constantly until well blended. When the batter gets too stiff to mix, turn out dough onto a lightly floured surface and knead by hand for 3 to 4 minutes. Shape into a loaf and press into a 4¹/₂-inch by 8¹/₂-inch loaf pan. Bake for 35 minutes or until loaf sounds hollow when turned out of the pan and tapped on the bottom. Brush with melted butter. Cool slightly on wire rack. Slice while still warm and serve with additional butter.
Makes 1 loaf.

Because corn was a source of life for Native Americans,
thanksgiving celebrations were held every summer for the
abundant crops of ripened ears. The tradition continues to this
day, and corn soup is usually featured as the main dish.

Iroquois Corn Soup

4 large white mushrooms, sliced

2 13^1/$_2$-ounce cans beef consommé

2 tablespoons yellow cornmeal

2 tablespoons minced cilantro

2 cloves garlic, crushed

2 tablespoons fresh basil, chopped

1 medium yellow onion, peeled and sliced

^{1}/$_2$ teaspoon freshly ground black pepper

Salt (to taste)

^{1}/$_2$ pound flounder fillets

1 10-ounce package frozen lima beans

^{1}/$_3$ cup dry sherry

In a large 12-inch saucepan, place the mushrooms, consommé, cornmeal, cilantro, garlic, basil, onion, pepper, and salt. Simmer over medium heat, uncovered, for about 10 minutes. Add the flounder, lima beans, and sherry, and simmer another 15 to 20 minutes, stirring occasionally and breaking the flounder into bite-size pieces. Serve piping hot.

Makes 4 to 6 servings.

Smoked Eel Stew

1 1^1/$_2$-pound smoked eel, cut into 2-inch pieces (Can substitute smoked cod or trout.)

7 very small potatoes, washed but not peeled, cut in half

2 cups pearl onions, peeled

3 large carrots, peeled, trimmed, and cut into julienne strips

4 to 6 cups fish stock

^{1}/$_2$ teaspoon freshly ground white pepper

Salt (to taste)

Combine all of the above ingredients in a heavy-duty 6-quart pot over high heat. Simmer 40 to 45 minutes, or until potatoes are tender. Skim off the excess fat. Serve hot with plenty of bread.

Serves 6.

Although there is a vast variety of edible
wild greens available in markets today,
the ingredients listed here for wild lettuce
salad were easily found by the Iroquois
and make a delightful combination.

Iroquoian Wild Lettuce Salad With Vinaigrette Dressing

1 cup scallions, finely minced

1 bunch watercress, trimmed and washed

**2 cups lamb's lettuce (mâche)
(Can substitute Bibb lettuce.)**

Combine the greens together in a large wooden salad bowl. Toss with Vinaigrette Dressing (recipe follows).

Serves 4 to 6.

Vinaigrette Dressing

$1/4$ cup safflower oil

2 tablespoons cider vinegar

2 teaspoons honey

$1/2$ teaspoon salt

Freshly ground pepper (to taste)

Put all ingredients in a bottle and shake vigorously before tossing with salad.

Corn Pudding

2 cups seedless raisins

3 cups scalded milk

$1^1/2$ cups light cream, chilled

1 cup cornmeal

$1/2$ cup molasses

1 teaspoon salt

$1/2$ cup granulated sugar

$1^1/2$ teaspoons ground ginger

$1/2$ teaspoon nutmeg

2 tablespoons melted butter

Preheat oven to 300°F. In a 2-quart saucepan, combine the raisins with the hot milk. In a separate bowl, add 1 cup of cold cream to the cornmeal. Stir into the hot milk over medium heat. Continue stirring for about 10 to 15 minutes or until the mixture starts to thicken. Mix in the molasses, salt, sugar, spices, and butter. Pour into a buttered 2-quart casserole. Then pour the remaining $1/2$ cup cream into the center of the pudding. Set the dish in a pan of cold water and put in a slow (300°F) oven for $2^1/2$ hours. Allow it to cool several hours before serving. Serve with sweetened whipped cream for an added treat.

Serves 6.

Kwanzaa

*Africa—with its breathtaking wildlife—is not just a land of exotic
flora and fauna; it's also an area steeped in tradition. During the
holiday of Kwanzaa, African-Americans pay homage to their
rich cultural heritage.*

Kwanzaa was initiated in 1966 by Maulana Karenga, Ph.D., a teacher of Black Studies who considered himself a cultural nationalist. Today it is recognized as a unique American holiday in which Americans of African ancestry can pay tribute to their rich cultural heritage.

Kwanzaa is observed from December 26 to January 1. The word itself means "the first" or "first fruits of the harvest" in the East African language of Kiswahili. Kiswahili was chosen primarily because it is a nontribal African tongue that seems to be popular over a large portion of the African continent. Another reason is that Kiswahili pronunciation is easy. Vowels are pronounced like those in Spanish, and the consonants, with a few minor exceptions, are like those in English. A is pronounced ah, as in father; E is pronounced a, as in way; I is pronounced ee, as in we; and O is pronounced oo, as in too. The accent is almost always on the next to last syllable.

The holiday called Kwanzaa is based on *Nguzo Saba* (The Seven Principles), which are used to enrich daily life. They include *umja* (unity) to maintain unity in the family, community, nation, and race as a whole; *kujichagulia* (self-determination) to define, name, create, and speak for themselves; *ujima* (collective work and responsibility) to build and maintain the community as a whole and to make all members of the community equally responsible for sharing each other's problems; *ujamma* (cooperative economics) to build and maintain their own shops and other businesses and to profit from them together; *nia* (purpose) to restore people of African ancestry to their traditional greatness; *kuumba* (creativity) to do as much as possible to preserve the community as it was inherited and to continue to make it a beneficial and beautiful place to live; and *imani* (faith) to believe in the righteousness of black people and their struggle.

Like many holidays, Kwanzaa is steeped in symbolism. The symbols of Kwanzaa are inspirational objects that reinforce principles, concepts, and practices that Karenga felt should be encouraged. There are seven of these symbols as well as two supplementary symbols that reflect traditional and modern concepts of Afro-American struggles. These seven symbols are: *mazao* (fruit and vegetables); *mkeka* (placemat); *kinera* (the candle holder for seven candles, one black, three green, and three red); *vibunzi* (ears of corn representing the number of children still in the home); *zawadi* (gifts); *kikombe cha umoja* (communal unity cup); and *mishumaa saba* (the seven candles).

The two supplemental symbols are the *Nguzo Saba* printed in large letters on a placard so that everyone can view them, and *bendara ya taifa,* which is the black, red, and green national flag developed by the father of the Black Nationalist movement, Marcus Garvey. The red symbolizes the blood his people shed, while green represents hope and the continent of Africa. Black is the color of the majority of its people.

The first symbol of Kwanzaa, *mazao,* is significant because it represents the rewards of collective productive labor. Kwanzaa was fashioned after the traditional celebrations that take place among African agricultural societies at harvesttime. The *mazao* represents the historical roots of the holiday itself. The *mkeka,* or placemat, is a symbol of tradition and is usually made from straw. The *kinera* is symbolic of the continental Africans who have come to represent their ancestors as a collective whole. *Vibunzi,* the ears of corn, represent children, and every family uses as many ears of corn during the celebration as they have children. This symbolizes the immortality of a fertile people. *Zawadi* are gifts that are given as a reward for commitments made and kept. They are usually exchanged among the immediate family to reinforce personal growth and achievement. The gifts are frequently books and handmade crafts, and there appears to be a real attempt to avoid commercialism.

During Kwanzaa, the celebrants fast from sunrise on the 26th to sunset on the 31st to cleanse both body and soul. They break their fast on the 31st with a feast called *karamu.* It is based on the seven principles of *Nguzo Saba,* with emphasis on *ujima, ujamma,* and *kuumba.* And it is a time in which an extremely economical meal—such as one of the following—is prepared collectively by the family or a group of friends.

▲▲▲▲▲▲▲▲▲▲▲▲▲▲▲▲▲▲▲▲▲

Kwanzaa

M E N U

Spicy Peanut Soup
Kwanzaa Fried Chicken
"African Togetherness" Health Salad
Nice Rice · Sweet Potato Pie

The heat of the African sun is conducive
to growing many different types of nuts.
Peanuts, a rich source of vitamin A
and protein, are quite prevalent in
African cuisine. This spicy peanut soup
demonstrates their versatility.

Spicy Peanut Soup

1 pound shelled, roasted peanuts

2 tablespoons butter

1 small onion

2 stalks celery, finely chopped

1 tablespoon curry powder

6 cups chicken broth

1 cup milk

1 cup heavy cream

1 teaspoon salt (or to taste)

1 teaspoon cayenne pepper (or to taste)

Chopped parsley for garnish

In a blender or food processor fitted with the metal blade, grind the peanuts to a fine consistency. In a large, heavy-duty saucepan, melt the butter. When hot, add onion, celery, and curry powder. Cook, stirring constantly, for 2 to 3 minutes until vegetables are softened. Add the ground peanuts and broth. Bring to a boil over high heat, then lower heat and simmer for 30 minutes. Add the milk and cream. Season with salt and cayenne pepper. Garnish with parsley.

Serves 6 to 8.

Cumin, coriander, cinnamon, and turmeric are just a few of the spices that make African cuisine rich in flavor.

Kwanzaa Fried Chicken

2 cups vegetable oil for frying

3 large eggs

¹/₂ cup buttermilk

¹/₄ cup freshly squeezed lemon juice

2 teaspoons salt

1 tablespoon freshly ground black pepper

2 tablespoons dried oregano

2 tablespoons powdered cumin

2 cups seasoned dry bread crumbs

2 3¹/₂- to 4-pound chickens, cut into 10 pieces

1 teaspoon baking powder

In a 12-inch skillet or in an electric frying pan, heat 1 inch of oil to 375°F or until a 1-inch cube of white bread browns in 1 minute. While the oil is heating, combine eggs, buttermilk, lemon juice, salt, pepper, and herbs in a medium-size bowl. Using a wire whisk, beat egg mixture until smooth and well blended.

Place bread crumbs and baking powder in a 1-gallon resealable plastic bag. Working with a few pieces of chicken at a time, dip first into egg mixture, letting the excess drip back into bowl, then place the chicken in the bag with bread crumbs. Seal the bag and shake until the pieces are well coated. If necessary, repeat this procedure. Place coated chicken pieces on a wire rack. When all the chicken is coated, carefully add enough chicken to the hot oil to fit in one layer without crowding. Cook, covered, 5 to 6 minutes on each side or until chicken is cooked through. Using tongs, transfer cooked chicken pieces to a cookie sheet lined with paper towels. If you plan to serve the chicken hot, keep it warm in the oven set on the lowest setting. Allow the temperature of the oil in the skillet to return to 375°F before frying the next batch of chicken pieces.

Serves 6 to 8.

*Although fried chicken is often associated with southern
American cuisine, it is also popular in Afro-American cooking.
Note the addition of cumin to the seasonings, which makes this
dish truly unique.*

*Root vegetables are very common in African cooking and are
important ingredients in many traditional recipes. In many
ways, it seems remarkable that such a hot climate produces such a
wide variety of produce.*

"African Togetherness" Health Salad

2 cups cooked bulgur wheat

1 large carrot, grated

3 minced scallions

1/2 cup seedless raisins

2 tablespoons sunflower seeds

1 cup broccoli florets, blanched

5 radishes, thinly sliced

1/2 cup fresh mint, chopped

Dressing:

1/2 cup plain yogurt

1/2 teaspoon salt

1/4 teaspoon cayenne pepper

2 teaspoons fresh thyme, chopped

1/4 cup fresh parsley, chopped

Juice from 2 lemons

1 head romaine lettuce

In a large bowl, combine bulgur, carrot, scallions, raisins, sunflower seeds, broccoli, radishes, and mint. Toss gently to combine. Chill for 1 hour. In a small mixing bowl, combine yogurt, salt, cayenne pepper, thyme, parsley, and lemon juice, and blend well. Just before serving, combine salad dressing with salad. Serve on romaine lettuce leaves.

Serves 6 to 8.

Nice Rice

1 cup long-grain rice

1 tablespoon butter

1/2 teaspoon curry powder

1/4 teaspoon turmeric

1/2 cup chicken broth

1/4 cup chopped scallions

In a 1-quart saucepan fitted with a lid, combine all the ingredients together, except the scallions. Bring to a boil. Cover, reduce heat to low, and simmer 25 to 30 minutes until all the liquid is absorbed and rice is tender but not mushy. Stir in chopped scallions.

Serves 6.

Sweet Potato Pie

4 medium-size yams, peeled and cut into 2-inch chunks

1/2 cup half-and-half

3 eggs

1/4 cup granulated sugar

4 tablespoons butter

1/2 teaspoon salt

1/2 cup shredded coconut

1/2 teaspoon nutmeg

1 teaspoon cinnamon

1 unbaked 9-inch piecrust

Preheat oven to 350°F. In a large pot over high heat, add yams and enough cold, salted water to cover. Bring to a boil, and cook until yams are quite soft, about 20 to 25 minutes. Drain in a colander. Add the yams to a large bowl, and mash well by hand with a fork or put them through a ricer or a food mill. Add half-and-half and blend in eggs. Mix in sugar, butter, and salt, and continue stirring until the butter has completely melted. Stir in coconut and spices. Pour this mixture into the prepared pie shell and bake 45 to 50 minutes or until a knife inserted into the center comes out clean.

Serves 8.

A Pennsylvania Dutch Folk Festival

Rolling hills dotted with well-tended livestock and fields of corn

color the Pennsylvania Dutch landscape. In the face of

modernism, the Pennsylvania Dutch farm as their ancestors did,

tilling soil that is as rich as their culinary tradition.

*a*lthough a frugal people, the Germans who settled in Pennsylvania—the Pennsylvania Dutch—have become known for the rich cuisine they prepare on feast days and at weddings and funerals.

Generally speaking, early Pennsylvania Dutch cooking should be classified by the preserving methods that gave each food its unique character. At least four processes of preserving were used in an attempt to find creative ways to store the succession of crops that came from field and garden to table: fermentation, drying, salting, and smoking. The early Pennsylvanian community was largely dominated by the wheat trade, so it should come as no surprise that yeast-raised breads—which use fermentation—and other baked goods became a specialty. And when these two items were combined, it was inevitable that fermented dough would become associated with Pennsylvania Dutch cookery.

Homemade yeast first was added to a variety of different types of flour. It was fermented in large troughs of wood, then transferred to straw baskets, where it was stored. From this yeast came the breads and raised cakes. One kind of unleavened bread, referred to as dunkard communion bread, was served at religious feasts. Here, each square of bread was marked with five nail prints symbolizing the five wounds of Jesus.

Raised cakes became associated with "dunking" and were called "coffee cakes." Some also were referred to as light cake, coffee wreath, funny cake, Moravian sugar cake, crumb cake, Schwenkfelder cake, and raised doughnuts, which were popular around Easter. These doughnuts were cut into squares or triangles, however, not into rounds with a hole in the middle as we see them today.

Two other popular items were pretzels and shoofly pie. The kind of pretzels that have become a popular snack food in the United States originated in the fifth century A.D. The dough—made of flour, water, coarse salt, and yeast—was twisted in such a way to represent two arms that are crossed in prayer. The name "pretzel," however, is a German contraction for the Latin word meaning "little arms."

In later years, pretzels took the place of bread during Lent in such countries as Austria, Germany, and Poland. So when pretzels were consumed they served as a reminder of the respect commanded by the season of Lent. In fact, they were such a symbol of Lent that they were often not eaten during any other time of the year.

Shoofly pies are another story. They are thoroughly Pennsylvanian, although the term "pie" is really a misnomer. It is actually a kind of poor man's cake made in earlier days with sorghum.

The most famous fermented food of the Pennsylvania Dutch, however, was sauerkraut. As soon as the cabbages matured in the garden, they were shredded and fermented in long earthenware crocks. Layers of shredded cabbage were alternated with salt, then compressed until the juices rose. This process was continued until the crock was full. Then it was covered with a cloth, weighted down with a round board and a number of rocks, and put in a warm place to ferment. After about a week or so, it was moved to a cool place. Two weeks later, the *kraut* was ready to be eaten.

The Pennsylvania Dutch also preserved foods by drying. Many different kinds of foods were dried, including beans, peas, and fruit. In fact, dried fruits make up some of the most characteristic flavors of such Pennsylvania Dutch dishes as *schnit und gneppe*—literally, dried apple slices and dumplings that were cooked with a hearty slab of bacon.

Game was also widely available, which helped to supplement domestic meats that were in limited supply. Women were largely responsible for butchering and then preserving or using the meats as

efficiently as possible. And they were efficient. With a pig, for example, every part of it was used except for the squell. The intestines were cleaned and used for making sausage. They also made scrapple—known as Philadelphia scrapple because of where it was sold—an old-time pork dish that wastes nothing. All scraps are put into use to make scrapple, including the cooking liquids.

The Pennsylvania Dutch were also quite innovative in commercial food preservation. They conceived the can and the jar, for example, which made the family garden virtually obsolete. The impact of cans and jars should not be underestimated, because they changed an agriculturally oriented economy into a commercially oriented one. Things like root cellars and bake ovens have practically disappeared because of these innovations.

Most of the Pennsylvania Dutch dishes were inherited from the Old World. Pies

were clearly the favorites—not only sweet pies but also savory ones like oyster, corn, and sorrel, which were meals in themselves.

But a second favorite was Christmas cookies. During Advent, all sorts of cookies were made and cut into various shapes—stars, shepherds, and animals of all kinds. Sometimes these were pressed on wooden forms known as *springerals,* a carryover from the Catholic custom where such dough creations were given as sacrificial gifts to the church.

If you'd like to get a real taste of Pennsylvania Dutch cooking, visit the Pennsylvania village of Kutztown during the first week of July. An authentic Pennsylvania Dutch Folk Festival—complete with old-time crafts, marriage ceremonies, and homemade shoofly pies—is held just outside of town every year.

Until you can get to Kutztown, however, here are a few recipes that capture the festival's flavor.

A Pennsylvania Dutch Folk Festival

M E N U

Biersuppe · Schnit und Gneppe

Philadelphia Scrapple

Bavarian-Style Red Cabbage with Apples

Shoofly Pie

The original settlers of Pennsylvania Dutch country were German, so it is little wonder that beer made its way into many of their recipes. The addition of cinnamon in this recipe for beer soup creates an unusual dimension.

Biersuppe *(Beer Soup)*

4 tablespoons sweet butter

2 tablespoons flour

4 cups Kronenburg or other German beer

¹/₄ teaspoon salt

¹/₄ teaspoon nutmeg

¹/₄ teaspoon cinnamon

4 egg yolks

1 tablespoon sugar

1 cup dry white wine

2 tablespoons grated lemon peel

Melt butter in a 2-quart saucepan. When hot, add flour all at once. Stirring constantly with a wooden spoon, cook for 2 to 3 minutes or until the mixture leaves the sides of the pot. While stirring, slowly pour in the beer. Add salt and spices. Simmer over low heat for 20 minutes. While the beer is simmering, beat the egg yolks well in a bowl, add the sugar, white wine, and lemon peel. Drop by drop, stirring constantly, add ¹/₄ cup of the hot beer into the egg mixture. Slowly stir the egg mixture into the remaining beer. Heat thoroughly without letting it reach a simmer. Taste and correct seasonings, if necessary. *Serves 6.*

Schnit und Gneppe

3 pounds ham butt

2 cups dried apples

$^1/_4$ cup dark brown sugar

1 egg, beaten

1 cup sifted flour

$^3/_4$ teaspoon baking soda

1$^1/_4$ teaspoons cream of tartar

$^1/_4$ teaspoon salt

2 tablespoons butter at room temperature

$^1/_2$ cup milk

In a large pot, combine ham with enough cold water to cover. Bring to a boil over high heat. Reduce heat to a simmer and cook about 1 hour or until the internal temperature measures 150° to 180°F.

Soak the dried apples in hot water for about 30 minutes or until soft. Add the apples with the brown sugar. Prepare the gneppe combining the egg with the sifted flour, baking soda, cream of tartar, and salt in a small bowl. Add butter and milk, mixing lightly. Twenty minutes before the ham is done, drop the gneppe batter by the tablespoonful into the simmering broth. Cover tightly and steam for 15 minutes. *Serves about 6.*

Philadelphia Scrapple

1 pound lean pork

3 pig's knuckles, split

2$^1/_2$ cups cold water

$^1/_2$ teaspoon thyme

$^1/_2$ teaspoon dried marjoram

1 teaspoon dried sage

2 teaspoons salt

1 teaspoon freshly ground pepper

1$^1/_4$ cups buckwheat

1$^1/_4$ cups cornmeal

$^1/_2$ cup all-purpose flour

2 cups vegetable oil for frying

Combine the meats with cold water in a large saucepan. Bring to a boil over high heat, reduce to a simmer, and cook until meat begins to fall off the bones, about 2 hours.

Remove meat from the bones and chop finely. Discard bones. Strain the broth and return 1 quart of the broth to the kettle. Reserve remaining broth and set aside to cool. Add the chopped meats and seasonings. Bring to a boil over high heat, then reduce heat to medium.

Combine buckwheat and cornmeal with the reserved, cooled broth. Pour into the saucepan with the meats. Stir the mixture until it's thickened, about 45 minutes to 1 hour. Remove the scrapple from the heat. Shape into a loaf and allow to cool. Slice it into $^1/_2$-inch-thick pieces, coat with flour on both sides, and fry in oil until golden. *Serves 6 to 8.*

Bavarian-Style Red Cabbage with Apples

¹/₄ pound bacon

1 large onion, chopped

1 tablespoon all-purpose flour

¹/₄ cup balsamic vinegar

¹/₂ cup dry red wine

¹/₂ teaspoon salt

¹/₄ teaspoon black pepper

1 2¹/₂- to 3-pound red cabbage, cored and shredded

¹/₂ teaspoon caraway seeds

1 Granny Smith apple, peeled, cored, and cut into ¹/₂-inch pieces

In a 12-inch heavy-duty or cast-iron skillet, cook bacon over medium-high heat until fat is rendered out. Remove bacon and reserve. Add the onion to the pan and cook, stirring, 3 to 5 minutes or until translucent. Sprinkle in the flour while stirring. Cook 30 seconds longer, then slowly pour in the vinegar and wine. Stir with a wire whisk to avoid lumps. Add remaining ingredients. Toss to mix well. Cover and cook for about 15 to 20 minutes—until cabbage is tender but not mushy.

Serves 6.

Shoofly Pie

³/₄ cup flour

¹/₂ cup dark brown sugar

¹/₂ teaspoon cinnamon

¹/₄ teaspoon ground nutmeg

¹/₄ teaspoon ground ginger

¹/₄ teaspoon cloves

¹/₂ teaspoon salt

2 tablespoons vegetable shortening

1 egg yolk, beaten

¹/₂ cup molasses

³/₄ cup boiling water

¹/₂ teaspoon baking soda

Prepared piecrust dough for a 9-inch pie, pre-baked

Preheat oven to 400°F. In a small bowl, combine flour, brown sugar, spices, salt, and shortening. Work into crumbs with your hands and put to one side. In another bowl, add egg yolk to molasses. Pour boiling water over the baking soda and add this to molasses mixture. Line a 9-inch pie plate with the pre-baked piecrust and fill with the mixture. Top with the crumb mixture and bake 10 minutes or until the crust is brown. Reduce temperature to 325°F and bake until firmly set, about 40 to 45 minutes.

Serves 6 to 8.

Aptly named, shoofly pie is a sugar pie—as difficult to keep away
from hungry folks as it is from flies.

A Mexican Fiesta

Some of the staple ingredients found in Mexican cooking—corn,
squash, and beans—have been growing in Mexican gardens for
more than 9,000 years. Today's Mexican fiestas offer a cuisine
that has been influenced by both the Aztecs and the Spanish.

*p*resent-day Mexican cuisine arose largely from Aztec and Spanish influences. To the native Aztecs' use of chocolate, vanilla beans, peanuts, tomatoes, achiote, chayote, avocados, corn, and chilies, the Spanish added oil, wine, cinnamon, cloves, rice, wheat, peaches, apricots, beef, milk, and butter. Of these, corn, chilies, and tomatoes are, today, the core of Mexican cuisine.

Sadly, chilies have been misunderstood and abused. They aren't just a volatile, macho food challenge. They are to Mexicans what herbs are to the French, and there are over 100 varieties in existence, varying in degrees of pungency, hotness, and all-around flavor. Most are divided into two groups: dried and fresh. The dried varieties are usually red. Exceptions are the red bell pepper and the heart-shaped pimiento, which are used fresh.

Chilies are used largely as a replacement for salt, although some old folklore associated with chilies tells of their healing properties as well as their ability to protect against disease, aid digestion, cleanse the blood, and encourage virility.

The levels of hotness are regulated by the removal of the seeds. Chilies should never make you feel as though you're breathing fire. Instead, they should just warm your palate and offer the food a unique flavor.

But Mexican cooking also means corn, beans, and squash—all three of which have been grown in Mexican gardens for over 9,000 years. Before the Spaniards, the Aztecs used chilies instead of salt; corn instead of wheat; bear suet instead of lard; ground nuts and seeds instead of butter; venison, rabbit, and wild birds instead of beef, chicken, and pork. They also leavened their bread with wood ashes instead of yeast.

The tortilla also has played an important role in Mexican cuisine. Not only is it a wrap for a variety of fillings but it also can be moistened and used to make dumplings. As with pasta, it is a component in quite a few casseroles. And when cut into triangles and deep-fried, it becomes a tortilla chip.

The burrito and the Mexican taco are two familiar dishes that use tortillas to enclose a variety of fillings. The burrito comes from northern Mexico and its tortilla is made from a wheat flour that is pale in color. The tortilla used to make the taco, on the other hand, is formed from yellow corn flour and is indigenous to the central and southern regions of the country. Both probably would be found at private family fiestas in their regions, along with one or two of the following recipes. And, of course, margaritas are de rigueur.

A Mexican Fiesta

M E N U

Guacamole · Arroz con Pollo
Classic Mexican-Style Savory Beans
Jicama Salad · Margaritas

Guacamole

4 large Haas avocados, peeled and pitted

Juice of 2 lemons

1 large onion, minced

5 large cloves garlic, crushed

1 to 2 jalapeño peppers, finely chopped

$1^1/_2$ teaspoons salt

$^1/_8$ teaspoon ground black pepper

$^1/_2$ cup finely minced cilantro

2 large ripe tomatoes, peeled, seeded, and chopped

In a large ceramic or glass bowl, mash the avocados lightly so they maintain a chunky consistency. Add lemon juice, onion, garlic, jalapeño pepper, salt, pepper, and cilantro. Blend well. Fold in chopped tomato. Transfer to a serving bowl. Cover with plastic wrap and refrigerate at least 1 hour before serving. Serve with corn tortilla chips.

Serves 8 to 10.

The ingredients used in guacamole can vary according to taste, but it should always be rich with the flavor of ripe, creamy avocados and lots of cilantro.

Arroz con Pollo

¹/₂ cup extra-virgin olive oil

1 3-pound chicken, cut into serving pieces

3 cloves garlic, crushed

1 large onion, minced

2 medium green bell peppers, finely chopped

1¹/₃ cups rice

1 tablespoon fresh chopped or 1 teaspoon dried oregano

¹/₂ pound piece Westphalian ham cut into ¹/₄-inch pieces

1 tablespoon salt

¹/₂ teaspoon freshly ground black pepper

2 teaspoons saffron threads

8 plum tomatoes, peeled and quartered

2 cups chicken broth

2 cups fresh or frozen peas

¹/₃ cup capers

Fresh parsley, chopped

Chopped pimientos

Traditional Mexican cuisine is virtually unknown to a large percentage of Americans—particularly since many ingredients are not readily available in most supermarkets. Arroz con pollo, however, is a popular dish that is easy to prepare.

Preheat oven to 350°F. In a large casserole dish, add oil over high heat. When hot, fry a few pieces of chicken at a time on both sides until golden, about 3 to 5 minutes. Remove chicken and reserve. In the same pan, sauté the garlic, onion, and green peppers until soft, about 5 minutes. Add the rice and stir to coat. Cook over moderate heat until just golden brown, about 3 minutes.

Return the chicken pieces to the casserole. Stir in the oregano, ham, salt, pepper, saffron, tomatoes, and broth. Bring to boil over high heat. Cover and place in the oven for 30 minutes. Reduce heat to 250°F. Add the peas and the capers. Continue baking, uncovered, until the chicken is tender, about 25 to 30 minutes. Garnish with parsley and pimiento.

Serves 8.

Classic Mexican-Style Savory Beans

1/4 pound pork rind

1/2 pound pink beans

1 small onion, thinly sliced

3 large cloves garlic, minced

1 bay leaf

6 cups beef broth or water

2 teaspoons salt

1/4 pound thick strips of bacon

2 medium tomatoes, peeled, seeded, and chopped

3 serrano chilies or jalapeños, seeded and finely chopped

1/4 cup finely chopped cilantro

In a large 8-quart saucepan, combine pork rind, beans, onion, garlic, bay leaf, and broth or water. Bring to a boil over high heat. Lower the heat, cover the pot, and allow the beans to cook gently for 1 1/2 hours. Add salt and cook another 15 minutes.

Cut the bacon into small pieces and cook in a medium-size skillet over high heat until golden brown. Add the tomatoes, chilies, and cilantro, and allow them to cook together over low heat, uncovered for 15 to 20 minutes. Add to beans. This can be eaten as a side-dish vegetable or, with the addition of more liquid, as a soup.

Serves 6 to 8.

Jicama, an unusual vegetable, might go unnoticed if it weren't for

its delightfully sweet, crunchy quality. Delicious both cooked and

raw, this recipe for jicama salad might be a nice introduction.

Jicama Salad

2 small jicamas (about 1¹/₂ pounds), peeled, sliced, and cut into julienne strips

¹/₄ cup crème fraîche

1 teaspoon salt

¹/₄ teaspoon freshly ground pepper

Juice of 1 lime

¹/₄ cup olive oil

3 small, sweet oranges, peeled and thinly sliced

¹/₄ cup fresh mint, chopped

Combine jicamas, crème fraîche, salt, pepper, lime juice, and olive oil. Blend well. Garnish with sweet oranges and fresh mint. Cover with plastic wrap and chill for at least 1 hour.

Serves 4 to 6.

Margaritas

2 thinly sliced limes

Salt (if desired)

12 ounces white tequila

4 ounces Triple Sec

8 ounces fresh lime juice (from about 20 limes)

Crushed ice

Rub the rim of 8 margarita glasses with a slice of lime. Dip the glasses into salt, if desired, pressing the rim of each glass deeply enough so that the entire rim is coated. In a large punch bowl, combine tequila, Triple Sec, and lime juice, and stir. Fill each glass with crushed ice and pour in margarita mixture.

Serves 8.

Perfect for a cocktail party, margaritas have that special south-of-the-border flavor just made to complement a bowl of zesty guacamole.

A Russian Vodka
and Zakuska Party

Because Russians love to entertain, it's been said that the center

of every Russian home is the table. The cuisine reflects both

peasant and noble roots; it is both elegant and down-to-earth.

Russian cuisine changed as radically as the social structure of its people after the 1917 October Revolution. When women began working outside the home, for example, the family was forced to develop a less complex type of cuisine because no one had time to prepare elaborate meals.

But the Russians, as a group, love to entertain. And, for the most part, the center of every Russian home is the table. No matter how small the dining room, there's always room for one more at the table.

Most often, the table is covered with a linen cloth and set with small plates, a series of shot glasses—*ryumochka*—for vodka, a glass for cognac, a goblet for wine, and a glass for juice or *kvass*, a home-brewed beer, or mineral water. Bottles of each are placed on the table at the beginning of the meal and remain there throughout.

The meal most often starts with a round of vodka, or cognac for those seeking a milder form of spirits. The shot glasses are filled almost to the top and the host proposes the first toast—usually to his guests. Then everyone clinks glasses and consumes the vodka in one shot. Russians do this because they believe that if you sip the vodka slowly, you'll get drunk faster because you're inhaling the fumes. (Another way of slowing the inevitable, Russians say, is to eat a piece of buttered bread after each shot of vodka.)

But aside from all the beverages, a Russian table is also laden with a variety of five to ten hot and cold *zakuski*—"little bites"—which are usually accompanied by white or rye bread. The white bread is considered the fancier of the two and is considered more appropriate for serving guests.

In season, there are usually a variety of sour-cream-based salads—beet vinaigrette and cucumbers in sour cream, for example—as well as pickled vegetables, canned sardines, marinated herring, sturgeon fil-lets, meat or vegetable-filled pies called piroshki, and, of course, caviar. And don't forget the stuffed eggs, beef kidneys in Madeira, Salade Olivier, and button mushrooms marinated in assorted spices and oil.

Depending on the occasion, these dishes can be as few as three or as many as twenty. Of course what pops to mind when considering the elements of a *zakuska* table is caviar or roe from the prized sturgeon that swim in Russian waters. The order of caviar from the highest grade to the lowest is beluga, oesetra, sevruga, sterlet, molossal, pressed (*pausnaya*) keluga, American, and lumpfish. To many, beluga is the only caviar worthy of being eaten. But sevruga is both delicious and reasonably priced.

Caviar should be served over ice in a silver or crystal bowl and spread with a gold, bone, or wooden spoon (any other material would interfere with the oily and delicate flavor of the caviar itself). And

although many aficionados love to eat caviar straight, it is also good served on toast points with crème fraîche or sour cream, chopped egg, minced onion, and fresh lemon. These accompaniments are considered an annoyance or interference by some, but there is no reason why anyone should feel the need to adhere to some sort of formula. Many Russians eat their caviar on plain or buttered white bread. So if anyone should look aghast at your doing the same, you can look them straight in the eye, eat your caviar, and rest assured that you are a lot more sophisticated and knowledgeable about this ritual than they are.

The beverage most linked to caviar is, of course, champagne. But according to the *New York Times,* a bubbly champagne interferes with the wonderful oiliness of the fish roe, and the article suggested that vodka might better complement the roe's distinctive characteristics. Being a champagne and caviar fan myself, I was skeptical, even though caviar and vodka has been a Russian tradition for centuries. But I shouldn't have raised an eyebrow. I tried it and found that caviar and vodka are a refreshing combination.

Russians love their vodka. The word is the diminutive of *voda*—"water"—the most basic of all elements. Not only is it good with caviar but it also provides the perfect balance to the frequently salty "little bites" of the *zakuska* table. A proper *zakuska* table should offer a variety of well-chilled vodkas in several flavors. These can be easily produced at home by making infusions of herbs, citrus peels, crushed cherry pits, or even saffron threads.

The best of the vodkas is *pshenichnaya*, which is distilled from grain rather than potatoes. It has a wonderfully pure, clean flavor and is rarely found outside of the Soviet Union. Other good Russian or Polish vodkas can be substituted satisfactorily, but American brands are thought, by some, to be raw and overwhelmingly alcoholic. They should never be endured straight. Russian vodka, however, is never drunk with the addition of mixers.

You should always keep vodka in the freezer. Its high alcohol content will keep it from freezing, and the cold will make the vodka so viscous that it will slide down your throat like melted butter.

A delightful way to entertain Russian-style is to set up a *zakuska* table, which should be oval or round so your guests can circulate freely. And although the "little bites" of *zakuska* are considered the Russian hors d'oeuvres, you could easily make a whole meal out of them.

Small plates, forks, and napkins are usually placed at opposite ends of the table so that people can serve themselves from both sides. Along the outer edge are placed the various *zakuski*—hot on one side, cold on the other. Toward the middle of the table should be plates or baskets piled high with both black and white bread. Plenty of unsalted butter—molded into fancy shapes—is placed alongside. In the center stand carafes of flavored vodka, surrounded by shot glasses.

You can add an entree—chicken Kiev and beef Stroganoff are Russian favorites—and follow it with a cup of tea and a selection of pies, cakes, chocolates, and sweetmeats, if you like. Fruit is frequently hard to obtain in the Soviet Union, so an authentic Russian dessert would be based on butter, flour, and/or eggs, rather than apples, oranges, and dates.

But why bother? On a cold winter evening, *zakuski* and vodka can start their own *perestroika* for both you and your friends.

A Russian Vodka and Zakuska Party

M E N U

Piroshki
Cauliflower and Turnip Crudité
Shashlik · Savory Beets
Marinated Smoked Salmon

Piroshki

Sour Cream Pastry:

3 ½ cups all-purpose flour

1 teaspoon baking powder

½ teaspoon salt

1 stick (4 ounces) sweet butter

2 large eggs, lightly beaten

½ pint sour cream

Mushroom Filling:

4 tablespoons sweet butter

6 minced scallions

¾ pound chopped mushrooms

1 tablespoon all-purpose flour

3 tablespoons crème fraîche

3 tablespoons fresh dill, chopped

2 hard-boiled eggs, chopped

½ teaspoon salt

1 teaspoon black pepper

⅛ teaspoon allspice

2 beaten eggs for glazing

Preheat oven to 400°F. In a large mixing bowl, sift the flour, baking powder, and salt. Cut the butter into the flour mixture until it is the consistency of coarse oatmeal. In another bowl, combine the eggs with the sour cream and beat until smooth, then blend this into the flour mixture. Knead the dough on a lightly floured board until smooth. Shape into a ball, cover, and chill 1 hour.

Melt butter in an 8-inch skillet over high heat. When hot, sauté scallions and mushrooms 3 to 5 minutes or until golden, then cook 1 to 2 minutes longer. Remove from heat, stir in crème fraîche, dill, chopped eggs, and seasonings. Mix well and reserve.

Roll out dough on a lightly floured surface to a ¼-inch thickness. Cut the dough into 3½-inch rounds. Place one heaping tablespoon of filling in the center of each round. Fold in half into crescents and crimp the edges with the tines of a fork to seal. Place the piroshki on a buttered baking sheet. Brush with the beaten egg and bake 25 to 30 minutes, or until golden brown.

Makes 2½ to 3 dozen.

The Russian zakuska, *or appetizer, can be as simple or as elaborate as the cook's time allows. A crudité (left) and piroshki (right) are typical offerings at a* zakuska, *but no matter what the dish, it is always followed by an icy cold glass of vodka.*

Cauliflower and Turnip Crudités

1 large head cauliflower, broken into florets and blanched

6 small turnips, peeled, sliced, and cut into $^1/_2$-inch strips

Dip:

3 large eggs, hard-boiled

2 teaspoons spicy-hot Russian-style mustard

1 pint sour cream

$^1/_4$ cup extra-virgin olive oil

$^1/_2$ teaspoon salt

$^1/_4$ teaspoon freshly ground black pepper

3 tablespoons chopped capers

2 tablespoons fresh parsley, chopped

Grate the eggs until finely minced. Combine with the remaining ingredients in a small serving bowl. Cover with plastic wrap and chill thoroughly, about 1 hour.

To serve, place serving bowl with dip on a large platter and arrange the vegetables around it.

Serves 6 to 8.

Shashlik

1 cup olive oil

1 cup red wine

¹/₂ cup freshly squeezed lemon juice

¹/₄ cup fresh dill, chopped

4 large cloves garlic, crushed

1 bay leaf

2 teaspoons ground black pepper

2 teaspoons salt

4 pounds boneless leg of lamb, cut into 1-inch pieces

32 small onions, peeled and parboiled

8 green bell peppers, seeded, cored, and quartered

In a large ceramic or glass bowl, combine oil, wine, lemon juice, dill, garlic, bay leaf, pepper, and salt. Mix well and add lamb. Cover bowl with plastic wrap and marinate overnight.

Preheat boiler or prepare charcoal grill. Drain lamb and reserve the marinade.

Thread skewers with marinated lamb, onions, and peppers, alternating the ingredients. Baste with marinade, then broil, turning once or twice during the cooking time, for 10 minutes or until desired doneness. Serve over rice.

Serves 6 to 8.

Shashlik was originally found in the area called the Caucasus. While lamb kabobs are found in many other countries, the addition of dill in this dish makes it uniquely Russian.

Savory Beets

3 tablespoons butter

1 medium onion, minced

2 pounds raw beets, peeled and grated

2 teaspoons grated lemon rind

¹/₄ cup freshly squeezed lemon juice

2 tablespoons flour

1 cup beef broth

1 teaspoon salt

¹/₂ teaspoon white pepper

¹/₄ cup fresh chives, chopped

¹/₄ cup fresh parsley, chopped

In a 12-inch skillet, melt butter over medium-high heat. When hot, add the minced onion and sauté 3 to 5 minutes or until translucent. Add the beets, lemon rind, and lemon juice. Reduce heat to low and cook until beets are just tender, about ¹/₂ hour to 45 minutes. Sprinkle with flour. Toss to coat and cook 1 to 2 minutes. Add beef broth and mix until well blended. Simmer, uncovered, about 10 minutes more. Remove from heat, season with salt and pepper, then add chives and parsley. The beets can be served hot or cold.

Serves 8.

Marinated Smoked Salmon

¹/₂ pound smoked salmon, thinly sliced

1 large red onion, sliced and separated into rings

10 black peppercorns, crushed

1 bay leaf, crumbled

¹/₂ teaspoon whole mustard seed

¹/₂ cup extra-virgin olive oil

¹/₂ cup safflower oil

¹/₂ cup champagne vinegar

3 to 4 medium cloves garlic, crushed

1 teaspoon salt

1 tablespoon capers

In a 1-quart mason jar fitted with a lid, alternate layers of smoked salmon, onion rings, (crushed) peppercorns, bay leaf, and mustard seed. In a medium-size bowl, combine the oils, vinegar, garlic, salt, and capers. Pour the dressing over the salmon. Seal the jar and allow to marinate for at least a week. Serve with black bread, butter, and lemon wedges.

Serves 8.

Smoked fish is one of the Russians' favorite foods, and marinated
smoked salmon is a special treat. The tanginess of the marinade
perfectly complements the smoky flavor of the salmon.

A Vietnamese Wedding

Vietnamese cooking, although largely influenced by the Chinese,
has a character all its own. Its popularity in the United States has
soared over the past decade, and at times, it has even been paired
with French cuisine to make a delightful union.

*V*ietnamese cooking has been influenced largely by the Chinese, but there is no mistaking one for the other. Vietnamese food has a character all its own.

Instead of using soy sauce, for example, a sauce called *nuoc mam* is served as an accompaniment to nearly everything. *Nuoc mam* is basically a liquid extracted from cooking fish. The Vietnamese add fresh chilies, garlic, sugar, and lime juice or vinegar until the flavor is much sharper and more pungent than anything Chinese cuisine has to offer. And with this sauce to display its national character, it's no wonder that food critics are beginning to call Vietnamese cooking the "nouvelle cuisine of the Orient."

Chilies play an important role in the seasoning of Vietnamese food, and if you're daring enough, it is more than acceptable to ask for a dish of freshly chopped chilies to increase the hotness of the dishes served. Unfortunately, if you've ever had the chance to eat Vietnamese food in America, its spicy qualities have probably been toned down to accommodate the Western palate.

Rice and noodles are the basic starches in Vietnamese cooking. Breakfast, for example, is usually noodle soup. It's rather overpowering by Western standards since fresh coriander, garlic, and *nuoc mam* play a part in its flavoring. And rice— accompanied by meat, poultry, or fish —is the basis of other meals.

Along with rice, however, soup is a major part of the Vietnamese meal. Sometimes, as with breakfast, soup is the entire meal. When it is, the type of soup—such as *pho,* the national soup of Vietnam—is usually fairly hearty. The long cooking time of *pho,* for example, results in a strong stock that is served with cooked noodles, raw vegetables, and a choice of raw or cooked beef. It's served as often as a cup of coffee is in the United States, but clearly it's a lot more nourishing.

Chicken, beef, duck, and pork are all found in Vietnamese cooking, but not lamb. Beef is considered a luxury so not too many recipes include it. Fish and shellfish are inexpensive and plentiful, so there are a lot of dishes that involve the cooking of fish. In fact, fish are so plentiful in Vietnam that they can even be found swimming in the flooded rice paddies. Some of these fish, referred to as "rice fish," are used in the making of *nuoc mam.* The fish are so small that they remind the Vietnamese of small grains of rice.

Salads are very popular in Vietnamese cooking, too. Simple combinations of cooked chicken or pork combined with cabbage, coriander, mint, *nuoc cham* (a sauce made with *nuoc mam*), and peanuts create wonderful explosions of flavor. Citronella, or lemongrass, is also used. Uncooked fresh fruit and vegetables are utilized in great quantities. And one of the most appealing things about Vietnamese cooking techniques is that the majority of the cooking is done in water.

A simple setting of bowls and chopsticks is used to prepare the table, and as with a Chinese meal, all the dishes are put on the table at one time. Everything is served in bowls. The bowl for rice and soup—which are frequently combined—is similar to a cup without handles. For whole meal soups, a larger bowl is used. Chopsticks are made of bamboo, ebony, and ivory. Bamboo chopsticks are the most common and the most likely to be used for family dinners. Ebony and ivory are the most expensive and are used for parties and special occasions. Chopsticks are placed to the right of the plate on top of the napkin. The soup spoon is usually made of stainless steel and is placed to the left of the plate. Dipping dishes—small shallow saucers or bowls about three inches in diameter—are placed at the top of the plate. There may be two or three or more of these, depending on the elaborateness of the meal.

The amount of time put into dinner for friends is an important indication of the respect and regard in which these friends are held. That's why rice is never served plain on special occasions but is specially prepared with extra ingredients for more color and flavor. Soups are more elaborate and use more expensive ingredients than usual and, unlike at family meals, are not served over rice.

When guests first arrive, they are served tea in the living room. From there they move into the dining room for a few appetizers and drinks, usually wine. The soup is then served, followed by the main dishes and a highly decorative rice dish. Dessert usually consists of fresh fruit. After dinner the guests will move back to the living room to finish the meal with tea.

One of the most important ceremonies in Vietnamese culture is the wedding ceremony. In America, a Vietnamese bride might wear the traditional Vietnamese red dress for the ceremony, then change into the traditional American white dress for the reception. Some of the classic dishes served at a Vietnamese wedding include Jade Hidden in the Mountain and Red Sweet (glutinous) Rice. Jade Hidden in the Mountain is a dramatic dish that is shaped into a multicolored mountain, its slopes lined with separate ingredients and its summit crowned by a flower (usually a chrysanthemum). An important member of the wedding party, usually a man, thanks the guests for attending, then removes the flower. And that's the signal for the festivities to begin.

Intrigued? Here are a few recipes to give any special dinner a Vietnamese flavor.

A Vietnamese Wedding

M E N U

Vietnamese Noodle Soup

Jade Hidden in the Mountain

Vietnamese Greens

Noodles are as much a staple in the Vietnamese diet as potatoes

are in the Irish. Not only are they served at special festive

occasions, but in this recipe, the chicken pieces can be left whole

and the soup can be served as a main dish.

Vietnamese Noodle Soup

2 8-ounce packages somen noodles

2 13¹/₂-ounce cans chicken broth

1 8-ounce can bamboo shoots, drained

2 chicken legs with thighs

1 tablespoon nuoc mam sauce (available in Asian grocery stores)

¹/₂ teaspoon salt

3 ounces dried black mushrooms, reconstituted in hot water and drained

1 tablespoon fresh coriander, minced

1 tablespoon minced scallions

Cook noodles according to package directions. Drain and reserve. Put chicken broth in a large pot over high heat, add bamboo shoots, and bring to a boil. Reduce heat to medium and simmer. Add chicken legs and thighs. Cover and cook 30 minutes or until chicken is tender. Remove from heat. Remove the chicken from the pot and allow it to cool slightly. Add *nuoc mam*, salt, and mushrooms to the broth. When the chicken is cool enough to handle, remove skin and shred meat into thin strips. Equally divide the chicken and reserved noodles into 6 to 8 bowls. Pour broth over each bowl and garnish with chopped coriander and scallions.

Serves 6 to 8.

Jade Hidden in the Mountain

Chicken Marinade:

1 teaspoon honey

1 tablespoon nuoc mam sauce

Chicken:

1 1/2 pounds boneless, skinless chicken thigh meat, marinated (see first step)

2 tablespoons vegetable oil

1 shallot, finely minced

2 cloves garlic, minced

Rice:

2 teaspoons vegetable oil

2 large cloves garlic, minced

2 cups minced onion

1 tablespoon imported tomato paste

2 cups long-grain rice

2 13 1/2-ounce cans low-sodium chicken broth

1 teaspoon granulated sugar

Egg Pancake:

2 teaspoons vegetable oil

3 large eggs, beaten

Salt and pepper (to taste)

Vegetables:

3 cups salted water

2 large carrots, peeled, trimmed, and cut into 1/4-inch cubes

2 cloves garlic, crushed

2 teaspoons vegetable oil

1 16-ounce can whole beets, rinsed and cut into 1/4-inch cubes

1 small green pepper, grated

1 cup green peas, fresh or frozen

Garnish:

1/4-pound piece cooked, boiled ham, cut into 1/4-inch cubes

1 fresh chrysanthemum, stemmed

Cut chicken into 1/4-inch strips and marinate in a combination of honey and *nuoc mam* for 1 hour.

To prepare rice, add vegetable oil to a 3-quart saucepan over medium-high heat. Stir in garlic and onions when oil is hot, cooking about 30 seconds. Add tomato paste and rice. Stir to coat. Add chicken broth and sugar. Increase to high heat. Bring to a boil and cover. Reduce heat to a simmer and cook 20 to 30 minutes, or until rice is just tender. Remove from heat and keep covered. Set aside while finishing the other elements of the dish.

In a 12-inch sauté pan, add teaspoons of the vegetable oil over high heat. When hot, add shallot and garlic. Cook, stirring rapidly, for 1 to 2 minutes. Add marinated chicken strips and cook 5 to 7 minutes or until cooked through. Remove from pan to a platter and reserve.

Wipe out sauté pan. Add 2 teaspoons vegetable oil over high heat. When hot, pour in beaten eggs and rotate pan to spread eggs into a single thin layer. Add salt and pepper to taste. Cook about 1 minute. Without folding the egg over onto itself, flip it over and cook about 1 minute longer. Remove from pan to a plate. Allow it to cool, then cut the egg into julienne strips. Set aside while cooking vegetables.

In a 2-quart saucepan, bring salted water to a boil over high heat. Add carrots and cook about 7 to 10 minutes or until tender. Drain and reserve.

In an 8-inch sauté pan, add 2 teaspoons oil over medium-high heat. When hot, add garlic and beets. Cook, stirring constantly, about 1 minute. Remove from heat and reserve.

Cook peas in boiling salted water about 3 to 5 minutes, or until tender. Drain and combine with the cooked rice, tossing gently.

Turn rice into a larger platter and shape into mountain peak. Arrange all the elements of the slopes (formed of vegetables and chicken) side by side, making certain to alternate the various colors. Top the mountain with the chrysanthemum to finish the dish.

Serves 8.

Jade Hidden in the Mountain is a classic dish, served at wedding ceremonies in southern Vietnam. A dramatic dish, it is shaped into a multicolored mountain with its slopes lined with different ingredients. An important member of the wedding party, usually a man, thanks the guests for attending and then removes the flower, the signal for the festivities to begin.

Vietnamese greens are used not only as seasonings in many
dishes, but can also be combined and eaten as a salad. Mint and
cilantro are two of the most predominant flavor enhancers, along
with lemongrass. The contrasting flavors create an exciting and
robust culinary experience.

Vietnamese Greens

1 cup shredded Chinese cabbage

2 cups shredded green leaf lettuce

2 tablespoons fresh chives, chopped

1/4 cup fresh cilantro leaves

2 tablespoons fresh mint, chopped

*1 large cucumber, peeled, seeded, and sliced
into 1/8-inch slices*

Dressing:

2 tablespoons nuoc mam

1/4 cup safflower oil

1 small clove garlic, minced

1/4 teaspoon red hot pepper sauce

Salt and pepper (to taste)

1/2 teaspoon sugar

Combine all the salad greens with the

dressing and toss well.

Serves 4 to 6.

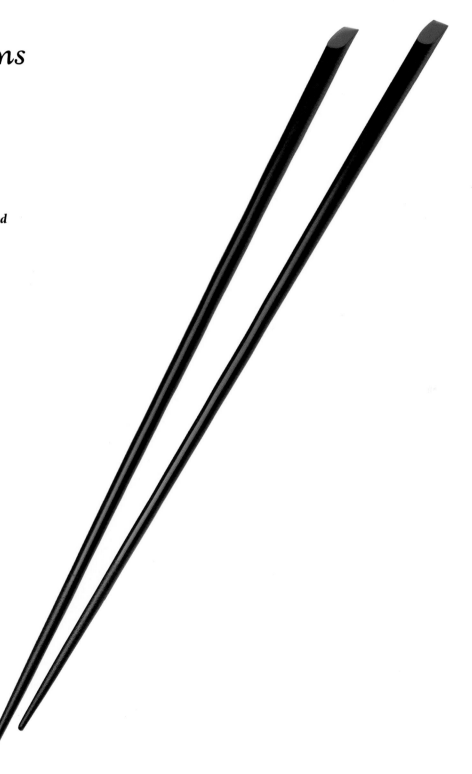

For Further Reading

Bayless, Rick and Deann A. *Authentic Mexican: Regional Cooking from the Heart of Mexico.* William Morrow, 1987.

Chu, Lawrence C. *Chef Chu's Distinctive Cuisine of China.* Harper & Row, 1988.

Frederick, J. George. *The Pennsylvania Dutch Cookbook.* New York: Crescent Books, 1989.

Goldstein, Darra. *A La Russe.* New York: Random House, 1983.

Gomez, Paulo. *Food in Mexico.* Rourke Corp., 1989.

Huong, Jill Nhu. *Vietnamese Cookery.* Miller Tuttle, 1968.

Lazar, Wendy. *The Jewish Holiday Book.* New York: Doubleday, 1977.

London, Ann, and Bishov, Bertha K. *The Complete American Jewish Cookbook.* Crowell, 1971.

McClester, Cedric. *Kwanzaa: Everything You Always Wanted to Know But Didn't Know Where to Ask.* New York: Gumbs & Thomas, 1985.

Munsen, Sylvia. *Cooking the Norwegian Way.* Minneapolis: Lerner Publications Co., 1982.

Nguyen, Chi, and Monroe, Judy. *Cooking the Vietnamese Way.* Minneapolis: Lerner Publications, 1985.

Pappas, Louis S. *Greek Cooking.* Harper & Row, 1973.

Prudhomme, Paul. *Chef Paul Prudhomme's Louisiana Kitchen.* New York: William Morrow, 1984.

St. Paul's Greek Orthodox Church Recipe Club. Hempstead (New York): Doubleday, 1981.

Sharpe, Edward J., and Underwood, Thomas B. *American Indian Cooking & Herblore.* Cherokee (North Carolina): Cherokee Publications, 1973.

Stern, Zelda. *The Complete Guide to Ethnic New York.* St. Martin's Press, 1980.

Tuuk, Van der, and Grunwall, Mariane. *Swedish Cooking at Its Best: Traditional and Modern Swedish Dishes.* Rand McNally, 1960.

Ulmer, Mary, and Beck, Samuel E. (editors). *Cherokee Cooklore: Preparing Cherokee Foods.* Published by Mary Goungback Chiltoskey.

Index

A

B

C

D

E

F

Additional photographs

All food photographs were styled by Cliff Ellman, a Los Angeles–based food/ prop stylist whose work has been widely published in books, magazines, and the advertising media. Jim Lape was the assistant food stylist. Photographer Lois Ellen Frank would also like to thank Carla Guimaraes, John Middlekoop, and Walter Whitewater for their assistance in the production of these photographs.

Props found on pages 15, 16, 18, 49, 50, and 52 were supplied by Primitive Instincts, Pasadena, California; pages 67, 68, and 71, Bullock's, Los Angeles, California; pages 75, 76, and 81, KATE, Santa Monica, California, and Ashbrook's, Santa Monica, California; pages 95, 96, 99, and 100, Barbara's Internazionale, Santa Monica, California, and Turkana, Los Angeles, California. The beadwork and leather found on pages 85, 86, 88, and 90 were supplied by AnnMarie Yazzie, Los Angeles, California. Food found on pages 131, 132, 135, and 137 was prepared by Lew Mitchell's Orient Express Restaurant, Lew and Louise Mitchell, Los Angeles, California. Props found on pages 30, 32, 33, and 34 were styled by Shaunah D. Smith.